KU-449-750

TOP 10
COPENHAGEN

ANTONIA CUNNINGHAM

EYEWITNESS TRAVEL

Left **Amalienborg Slotsplads** Right **Houses along Nyhavn**

LONDON, NEW YORK,
MELBOURNE, MUNICH AND DELHI
www.dk.com

Reproduced by Colourscan, Singapore
Printed and bound in China by Leo Paper
Products Ltd

First published in Great Britain in 2007
by Dorling Kindersley Limited
80 Strand, London WC2R 0RL
A Penguin Company

**Copyright 2007, 2011 © Dorling
Kindersley Limited, London**

Reprinted with revisions 2009, 2011 (001)

A CIP catalogue record is available from
the British Library.

ISBN 978 1 40535 886 6

Within each Top 10 list in this book, no
hierarchy of quality or popularity is implied.
All 10 are, in the editor's opinion, of
roughly equal merit.

MIX
Paper from
responsible sources
FSC
www.fsc.org   FSC™ C018179

Contents

Copenhagen's Top 10

Left **Interior of Vor Frue Kirke** Right **Kunstindustrimuseet**

Left **New Year fireworks at Tivoli** Right **Café culture on Nytorv**

Key to abbreviations
Adm *admission charge* **Dis Access** *disabled access*

COPENHAGEN'S TOP 10

🔟 Copenhagen's Highlights

A kaleidoscope of history, culture and contemporary entertainment, Copenhagen is a vibrant capital city offering an incredible array of experiences. Walk through the cobbled streets of an ancient city, explore world-class museums, experience the finest restaurants and hippest nightlife, or simply unwind beside the gorgeous waters of a peaceful seaside town. Copenhagen has a compact centre that can easily be seen on foot and is also a great city for cycling. Voted "Europe's Coolest City" by design magazine Wallpaper, this charming destination has something for everyone.

Harbour Sights ⬛1
The best way to soak in the city's plentiful and beautiful harbour sights is to take a harbour trip, from Nyhavn through the Inner Harbour, along the canals of Slotsholmen and Christianshavn. It is also a fantastic way to understand Copenhagen's development over the years *(see pp8–9)*.

Tivoli ⬛2
This pleasure garden and fun fair attracts kids and adults alike. At night, it turns especially magical with sparkling fairy lights and Chinese lanterns. The rides are brilliant for an adrenaline rush and if you feel peckish, head to one of the many restaurants *(see pp10–13)*.

Rosenborg Slot & Kongens Have ⬛3
Set amid one of Copenhagen's prettiest parks, this 17th-century Renaissance castle houses the royal collection, including the spectacular Crown Jewels in the basement *(see pp14–15)*.

The Latin Quarter ⬛4
One of the oldest areas in Copenhagen, the Latin Quarter is just off the main pedestrianized street, Strøget. It is home to the university and the few medieval buildings in the city *(see pp16–17)*.

Preceding pages: **Colourful houses lining Nyhavn.**

5 Kongens Nytorv and Nyhavn

Kongens Nytorv (King's New Square) is a splendid Baroque square that leads down to Nyhavn. Previously a seedy haunt for sailors, complete with drinking dens and brothels, it has transformed radically in recent times. Today, this scenic area is a popular waterside attraction with plenty of restaurants and bars *(see pp18–19)*.

6 Amalienborg

Home to the royal family since 1794, this complex of palaces represents some of the best Rococo architecture in Denmark. The museum housed in Christian VIII's palace has some fascinating displays *(see pp20–21)*.

7 Statens Museum for Kunst

You will find a wonderful collection of Danish and European sculpture and paintings at the national gallery. It is set inside a 19th-century building, connected by a glass bridge to a modern wing. There is also a large green park behind the museum *(see pp22–3)*.

8 Ny Carlsberg Glyptotek

This fabulous, renovated and extended museum is a definite must-see. It includes wonderful ancient Egyptian, Roman and Mediterranean works of art. The new wing boasts an impressive collection of French Impressionist and Post-Impressionist art *(see pp24–5)*.

9 Nationalmuseet

Here is a perfect example of how brilliantly the Danes design their museums. Formerly a palace, the museum *(left)* houses collections devoted to Danish history. You will also find fabulous ethnographic artifacts from around the world, as well as an excellent children's museum *(see pp26–7)*.

10 Slotsholmen

This is where it all began in the 12th century, when Bishop Absalon built a castle here (you can still see its remains). The present Neo-Baroque castle was built in 1907–28, but was never in-habited by the monarch. It is now shared between the Royal family and the Parliament *(see pp28–9)*.

🔟 Harbour Sights

A harbour tour is a delightful way to take in the city's brilliant views and varied topography. You will be taken along the wide waters of the Inner Harbour, winding waterways of Christianshavn and round to Slotsholmen (the island on which the original town of Havn flourished in the 12th century). Vor Frelsers Kirke, in particular, makes a spectacular sight as you look up through the rigging of sailing boats dotting the Christianshavn canal.

Den Sorte Diamant
The Black Diamond, an eye-catching, vast, shiny structure, holds all the books ever published in Denmark (4.5 million) – the biggest collection in Europe. It is a great place to check out original Danish texts.

Operaen

⏱ DFDS and Netto Boats offer guided canal and harbour tours. You can forego the commentary and the canals by taking a yellow public transport Harbour Bus (901/902) from Den Sorte Diamant, Knippelsbro, Nyhavn, the Opera House, Nyholm or Larsen Plads. Copenhagen Cards are accepted *(see p111)*.

• Map L4 • DFDS Canal Tours: 32 96 30 00; open 10am–5pm; adm for adults 60kr, children 40kr; boats every 30 mins; tours in English, French, Danish, German, Italian and Spanish; www.canaltours.com
• Netto Boats: 32 54 41 02; open 10am–5pm Mar–Oct (Oct–Mar Sat–Sun only); adm for adults 30kr, children 15kr; boats 2–5 times an hour; tours in English, German and Danish; www.netto-baadene.dk

Top 10 Attractions
1. Operaen
2. Nyhavn
3. Den Sorte Diamant
4. Langelinie
5. Havnebadet
6. Little Mermaid
7. Trekroner
8. The Canals
9. Houseboats
10. Pavilions and the Royal Yacht

Operaen
The incredible Opera House *(above left)* was built in just four years. Its massive, orange-maple coloured auditorium seats 1,700 people. The amazing sculptures in the foyer change colour with the weather.

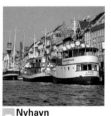

Nyhavn
Even today, the charming old harbour of Nyhavn is filled with boats. The old brothels and pubs have now been turned into respectable bars and restaurants serving traditional Danish dishes.

Langelinie
One of Copenhagen's most scenic areas, this is a wonderful place to walk along the harbour banks. Stroll past Kastellet and the Little Mermaid, right up to the final stretch – the longest cruise ship pier outside Miami *(below)*.

Inderhavnen (Inner Harbour) runs through central Copenhagen; Øresund (the Sound) separates Denmark and Sweden.

5 Havnebadet

Take a refreshing dip in the sparkling clean harbour waters of this popular open-air pool, while enjoying superb views of the city. Located at Island's Brygge, there are three pools to choose from – for adults, children and a pool for divers. They are separated from each other and from the harbour waters by floating bridges.

6 Little Mermaid

Den Lille Havfrue is a surprisingly small landmark, commissioned by the brewery magnate, Carl Jacobsen in 1909. It was created in 1913 by Edvard Eriksen, whose wife, Eline, was the model.

7 Trekroner

This 18th-century fort has been used only once: on 1 April 1801, during the Battle of Copenhagen when firing against the British fleet. Second in command at that time was Admiral Lord Nelson.

8 The Canals

The canals that you glide along on the tour (above), were built in a Dutch style in 1618 at the command of Christian IV. It is because of this that Christianshavn is sometimes also referred to as "Little Amsterdam".

9 Houseboats

The houseboats along the canals have an eclectic mix of styles, ranging from the conventional boat-like structures, to some with barge-like designs and other modern, funky homes built on floating platforms, complete with outdoor spaces.

10 Pavilions and the Royal Yacht

On the quayside, just beyond the Little Mermaid, are two green pavilions (below). It is here that the Danish royal family gathers before boarding their stunning, 79-m (259-ft) royal yacht, called the Dannebrog, also the name of the Danish flag, which is said to have fallen from the sky in the year 1219. Launched in 1931, the yacht is crewed by nine officers, seven sergeants, and 36 seamen: an improvement on the earlier royal ship, a paddle steamer dating back to the year 1879.

Mutant Mermaid

Close to the Little Mermaid, practically inviting controversy, sits a collection of sculptures called Paradise Genetically Altered. It comprises a triumphal arch, with a 9-m (29-ft), genetically altered Madonna atop it, surrounded by Adam, Eve, Christ, Mary Magdalene, The Tripartite Capital and The Pregnant Man. It is a surreal take on the Little Mermaid perched a short distance away. Designed by Bjørn Nørgaard, it is a comment on the modern human condition.

 For hotels with water views, see p117; and for days out by the Sound, see pp96–103.

Tivoli

Famous for its fairy-tale ambience, exotic buildings, gorgeous landscaped gardens and upmarket entertainment and restaurants, the Tivoli Gardens are more than an amusement park. The atmosphere is magical enough to merit a visit even if you are not interested in the excellent rides on offer. Founded in 1843, Tivoli has long been a favourite with royalty. It also proved to be a great source of inspiration for Walt Disney when he visited in 1950.

1 Thrill Rides

Day or night, Tivoli ring with the shrieks of people whizzing along on the high speed thrill rides, such as *The Dragon*, *The Demon*, *Vertigo* and *The Starflyer*, the world's tallest carousel

Tivoli Gardens

🎠 Go on the thrill rides during the day when it's more family-oriented, since queues can build up in the evenings.

🍴 Enjoy a meal at one of the restaurants here *(see pp12–13)*.

- Map H5
- Vesterbrogade 3
- 33 15 10 01
- Open mid-Apr–Sep 11am–11pm Mon–Thu & Sun, 11am–12:30am Fri, 11am–midnight Sat
- Adm for adults 95kr; children 50kr; free for under-3s
- Dis access
- www.tivoli.dk

Top 10 Features

1. Thrill Rides
2. Gentle Rides
3. Traditional Rides
4. Dragon Boats
5. Tivoli at Night
6. Pantomime Theatre
7. Tivoli Concert Hall and Open-Air Stage
8. Tivoli Akvarium
9. Tivoli Boys' Guard
10. Nimb Hotel

2 Gentle Rides

For children and the faint-hearted, there are plenty of fun, gentle rides. *The Ferris Wheel* is an observation wheel that offers great views over Tivoli. You could also enjoy an old-fashioned trolley bus ride, a traditional carousel with exotic animals and music, a merry-go-round in the shape of a pirate ship and several charming kids' rides, such as flying aeroplanes and miniature classic cars.

3 Traditional Rides

Tivoli's current Ferris Wheel dates from 1943. *The RollerCoaster* (1914), the oldest wooden construction, reaches speeds of 36 mph (58 km/h).

4 Dragon Boats
These boats are very popular rides at Tivoli. Kids love floating on the lake during the day. In the evenings, the setting turns romantic.

5 Tivoli at Night
Sparkling resplendently with thousands of fairy lights and Chinese lanterns, Tivoli is magical at night. You can catch the dazzling *son-et-lumière* presentation and the exuberant Tivoli Iluminations, a late-night presentation over the lake.

6 Pantomime Theatre
Built in 1874, this theatre has an exotic Chinese design and a spectacular stage curtain styled like a peacock's tail *(left)*. It is known for its enjoyable mime shows, performed in the commedia dell'arte tradition.

7 Tivoli Concert Hall and Open-Air Stage
This Concert Hall hosts varied performances, from classical music to pop concerts. The open-air stage holds free rock concerts on Friday nights.

8 Tivoli Akvarium
Don't miss the amazing aquarium in the foyer of the Concert Hall. Based on a tropical coral reef, it is the longest salt water aquarium in Denmark and is home to 1,600 fish (over 500 varieties). Among the popular attractions are the rays and the enormous eels.

9 Tivoli Boys' Guard
A tradition since 1844, the Boys' Guards parade through Tivoli, complete with instruments, coach and horses – a delightful picture, befitting the home city of that master of fairy tales, HC Andersen.

10 Nimb Hotel
This splendid hotel, housed in the Nimb building *(above)*, offers a variety of culinary experiences, such as a *vinoteque*, Andersen Bakery, a grill with home-made hotdogs, a gourmet restaurant and a dairy.

Christmas at Tivoli
Tivoli opens for six weeks between mid-November and the end of December for a winter wonderland; a no-holds-barred, elf-driven, Father Christmas-strewn, illuminated Christmas extravaganza that you won't forget in a hurry! A similar Halloween celebration takes place in mid-October.

For more places that children will enjoy, see pp56–7.

Left **The Paul restaurant** Centre **Café Ketchup** Right **Café Ultimo**

🔟 Tivoli Restaurants

1 The Paul
This Michelin-starred restaurant, set in a lovely Winter Garden, is run by award-winning chef Paul Cunningham. Its six-course set menu for lunch and dinner changes regularly and includes dishes like creamed truffled pasta. ⬡ 35 75 07 75 • www.thepaul.dk • ⑧⑧⑧⑧⑧

2 Nimb Brasserie
Nimb Brasserie provides informal, up-scale dining that's less exclusive than upstairs at Hermans (see p48). Contemporary Danish cuisine is prepared in the centrally placed open-plan kitchens. ⬡ Bernstorffsgade 5 • 88 70 00 10 • Open 11:30am–11pm daily • www.nimb.dk • ⑧⑧⑧⑧

Det Japanske Tårn

3 Café Ultimo
Italian cuisine is served in this pretty, circular building that was originally built as a dance hall in 1883. ⬡ 33 75 07 51 • www.cafeultimotivoli.dk • ⑧⑧⑧

4 Café Ketchup
Styled like a Parisian bistro, this lovely restaurant, formerly a 19th-century tea room, offers a variety of tantalizing fusion dishes and traditional Danish fares too. The lunch menu comes from Ida Davidsen (see p79). ⬡ 33 75 07 55 • www.cafeketchuptivoli.dk • ⑧⑧⑧⑧

5 Divan 2
Along with Café Ketchup (formerly Divan I), this is one of the oldest and best restaurants in Tivoli, offering excellent Danish delicacies. It has played host to Queen Elizabeth II, Jimmy Carter, Henry Kissinger and Indira Gandhi. ⬡ www.divan2.dk • ⑧⑧⑧⑧

6 Det Japanske Tårn
This exotic Tivoli icon on the lake makes a spectacular picture, especially when it is lit up at night. The former Chinese Tower offers sushi, teriyaki and other Japanese and Asian cuisine. ⬡ 33 33 78 00 • ⑧⑧

7 Færgekroen Bryghus
Færgekroen, one of Tivoli's oldest restaurants, has been made over into a modern space, with its own brewery. The rustic charm has been preserved, while the traditional Danish food complements the fine ales. ⬡ 33 75 06 80 • www.faergekroen.com • ⑧⑧⑧

8 Wagamama
One of Copenhagen's cheapest restaurants, this trendy chain offering excellent Japanese fare is situated in the complex at the Tivoli Concert Hall. It can get very busy, so you may find yourself sharing a table with strangers. ⬡ 33 75 06 58 • www.wagamama.dk • ⑧

For a key to the price categories, **see pp67, 71, 79, 87, 93 and 103.**

9 Hereford Beefstouw

The flagship restaurant in a chain of upmarket steakhouses, the Hereford Beefstouw is a mecca for people who love beef and beer. The steaks are cooked just right and are of first-class quality with prices to match. Its micro-brewery, the Apollo, stands right in the centre of the restaurant.

Stegt Flæsk

🏵 *Vesterbrogade 5* • *33 12 74 41*
• *Open 11:30am–3pm & 5:30pm–10:30pm Mon–Sat, 5pm–10:30pm Sun*
• *www.a-h-b.dk/tivoli* • ⊛⊛⊛

10 La Vecchia Signora

This cheerful Italian restaurant is well known for its stone-oven-baked pizzas, all produced in traditional ovens specially imported from Sardinia, Italy. The rest of the menu includes home-made pasta topped with a variety of sauces, *carpaccio*, mussels in parsley and garlic, fresh fish of the day, meat dishes and authentic Italian puddings. 🏵 *33 75 09 75*
• *Children's menu available* • ⊛⊛

Top 10 Historic Events

1. 1843: Tivoli opens with a horse-drawn carousel and a roller coaster.
2. 1944: The Nazis blow up part of Tivoli in order to crush Danish morale.
3. 1950: Walt Disney visits Tivoli and is inspired to create his own park.
4. 1956: The Concert Hall is inaugurated, the largest one in Northern Europe at the time.
5. 1978: The New York City Ballet and its founder, George Balanchine, visit.
6. 1990s: Michael Jackson performs at Tivoli and offers to buy it.
7. 1994: Tivoli's Christmas season is launched.
8. 2000: Hosts the 60th birthday celebrations for the Queen.
9. 2003: The Paul, Tivoli's first Michelin-starred restaurant, opens.
10. 2006: Launch of *The Starflyer*, the world's tallest carousel.

The Founding of Tivoli

The creation of the Tivoli Gardens can be credited to Georg Carstensen, a man who persuaded the Danish king, Christian VIII, to grant him a five-year charter by saying, "When the people are amusing themselves, they do not think about politics." Mindful of this fact, Christian VIII granted him 6 ha (15 acres) of land outside the city walls. Carstensen, who had been brought up in the Middle East, provided oriental-style buildings, cafés, restaurants and in the early days, a horse-drawn carousel and a roller coaster. Brilliant fireworks further enlivened this magnificent amusement area. It was named Tivoli after the Jardins de Tivoli in Paris, which were themselves named after a place called Tivoli just outside Rome. The gardens inspired Walt Disney greatly when he visited; in fact, he was so impressed by them he once exclaimed to his wife, "Now this is what an amusement place should be!"

Tivoli at night

For more restaurants in the Tivoli area, see pp67 and 71.

ⁱ⁰ Rosenborg Slot and Kongens Have

Complete with fairy-tale turrets and stone lions guarding the entrance, the Rosenborg Castle was originally built as a summer house in 1606–34 by Christian IV. At that time, it stood surrounded by sprawling gardens (now the Kongens Have park) out in the tranquil countryside. This was Christian IV's favourite castle and like other monarchs after him, he used it as his main residence. When he was on his deathbed at Frederiksberg Castle in 1648, he insisted on being brought to Rosenborg Castle, and eventually died here.

Rosenborg Slot

⚙ Avoid lurking near the guards at the entrance to the Crown Jewels – you might be considered a security risk.

🍴 There is a restaurant and a small café in Kongens Have, but you will enjoy yourself a lot more if you have a picnic on the lawn or on one of the many benches in the garden.

• Map J2
• Øster Voldgade 4A
• 33 15 32 86
• Open Nov–Apr 11am–4pm Tue–Sun; May, Sep & Oct 10am–4pm daily; Jun–Aug 10am–5pm
• Adm for adults 65kr, students and senior citizens 40kr, free for under-17s; Kongens Have gardens free; Copenhagen Card accepted (see p111)
• Guided tours (1–1.5 hr long) in English, German and French
• museum@dkks.dk
• www.rosenborgslot.dk

Top 10 Features

1 Rosenborg Slot
2 Crown Jewels
3 The Winter Room
4 Christian IV's Bedroom
5 The Dark Room
6 The Marble Hall
7 Frederik IV's Chamber Room
8 The Rosen Antechamber
9 Knight's Hall
10 Kongens Have

ⁱ Rosenborg Slot
The castle's 24 rooms occupy three floors. Most of them retain the original Renaissance decor from Christian IV's residence, while the rest have been redecorated by later kings. The last king to live here permanently was Frederik IV. The castle is unique for its museum tradition, and opened to the public as early as 1838.

² Crown Jewels
The castle has been used as the treasury of the realm since 1658. In the castle's basement, behind heavily-guarded security doors, are Denmark's Crown Jewels *(above)*, that include Christian IV's diamond-encrusted crown, pearls and enamel figures.

³ The Winter Room
This panelled room was said to be one of Christian IV's most important private chambers. Look out for the intriguing speaking tubes that connect with the wine cellar and room above.

⁴ Christian IV's Bedroom
Another private apartment, Christian IV's bloodied clothing, from the naval battle of Kolberger Heide (1644) where he lost an eye, are found here. The king wanted these clothes preserved as national mementos.

5 The Dark Room
This room is filled with fascinating objects, such as the startling wax portraits of the Absolute monarchs, and the 17th-century "trick" chair that grasped unsuspecting occupants with tentacles and soaked them in water. A trumpet played when they finally stood up.

7 Frederik IV's Chamber Room
In the 1700s, this room was used by Frederik IV's sister, Sophie Hedvig, as an antechamber and the tapestries date back to this period. Look for the intricate equestrian statue of Frederik, made from ivory, wood and tortoise shell. The coffered ceiling *(below)* is the original from the time of Christian IV.

8 The Rosen Antechamber
An extraordinary room with glowing gold leaves and tooled leather on the walls, it has undergone restoration to look exactly as it did before the royal family moved to Frederiksberg Slot around the 1740s. The room's square shape has since been restored and the fittings, ceiling paintings and wall decorations were brought back from Frederiksberg Slot.

9 Knight's Hall
Known as the Long Hall before 1750, this room was completed in 1624 as a celebration hall. Only two Dutch fireplaces remain from the original decorations. Note the beautiful white stucco ceiling, Frederik III's astonishing unicorn horn throne (1660s), guarded by silver lions, and the solid-silver, Baroque furniture.

10 Kongens Have
Visited by over two million people every year, these are Denmark's oldest royal gardens and date back to the 17th century. There is a rose garden, Staudehaven, which contains many statues, including one of Hans Christian Andersen and a large one of Queen Caroline Amalie that was created by Vilhelm Bissen. Enjoy a lovely long walk on the pathway that passes through the flowerbeds. Also at the park is the Renaissance garden, Krumspringet. Art events and a puppet theatre for children are held here during summer.

Rosenborg's Kings

Christian IV, 1588–1648: Built many of Copenhagen's Renaissance buildings.
Frederik III, 1648–1670: Introduced Absolute Monarchy to curb the aristocracy's power.
Christian V, 1670–1699: Introduced fairer taxation.
Frederik IV, 1699–1730: Built Frederiksberg Castle, among other well-known buildings.
Christian VI, 1730–1746: Known as the religious king.
Frederik V, 1746–1766: Responsible for the building of the Frederiksstaden district.

6 The Marble Hall
Originally the bedroom of Kirsten Munk, Christian IV's morganatic wife, Frederik III turned it into a Baroque show of splendour *(below)* to celebrate the introduction of Absolute Monarchy.

For more royal sights, see pp58–9.

🔟 The Latin Quarter

The Latin Quarter is home to Copenhagen's university, where Latin used to be the spoken language. One of the oldest areas in the city, it is full of 17th-century buildings that were built by the architect king, Christian IV. Although there have been dwellings here since medieval times, most of them were destroyed in the disastrous fire that spread across Copenhagen in 1728 (see p33). Today, the Latin Quarter is a lively and bustling student area brimming with shops and cafés.

Universitetet

🕐 This area is known for its hip, alternative shops.

🍴 Studenterhuset, opposite Regensen, is a cheap option.

• Map H4
• Helligåndskirken: Niels Hemmingsensgade 5; 33 15 41 44; open noon–4pm Mon–Sat.
• Synagogen: Krystalgade 12; 33 12 88 68
• Rundetårn, Trinitatis Kirke: Købmagergade 52A; 33 73 03 73; Tower: open Jun–Aug 10am–8pm Mon–Sat, noon–5pm Sun; Sep–May 10am–5pm Mon–Sat, noon–5pm Sun; www.rundetårn.dk Church: open 9:30am–4:30pm Mon–Sat; www.trinitatiskirke.dk
• Universitetet: Nørregade 10; 35 32 26 26; open 9am–5pm daily; www.ku.dk/english/
• Vor Frue Kirke: Nørregade 8; open 10am–noon Mon–Sat
• Sankt Petri Kirke: Skt Peders St 2; 33 13 38 33; open 10am–noon Sun

Top 10 Features

1. Helligåndskirken
2. Synagogen
3. Rundetårn
4. Universitetet
5. Trinitatis Kirke
6. Vor Frue Kirke
7. Sankt Petri Kirke
8. Regensen
9. Højbro Plads
10. Gråbrødretorv

Helligåndskirken
The Church of the Holy Ghost *(below)* was originally part of a monastery built in 1296 and dissolved in 1536. The Helligåndshuset, the monastery's west wing, is the city's only preserved medieval building.

Synagogen
Built in 1833, this is Copenhagen's oldest synagogue, and one of the few in Europe to have survived Nazi occupation. The main synagogue for the city's Jewish community, it is not open to visitors.

Rundetårn
The Round Tower was built in 1642 by Christian IV as an observatory, its official role till 1861. It is 34.8 m (114 ft) high, with a wide internal ramp that spirals almost to the top *(below)*. It is open to the public and holds temporary art exhibitions and classical concerts.

Tsar Peter of Russia supposedly rode his horse to the top of the Rundetårn in 1715, his wife following in a coach and six.

4 Universitetet

Founded in 1479 by Christian I, the University of Copenhagen was Denmark's first university. The Neo-Classical building that stands here today is from the 19th century. In the courtyard, there are the remains of an old Bishop's Palace (1420). Disorderly students used to be put in its cellar as punishment. Most of the university is now on the island of Amager.

5 Trinitatis Kirke

This magnificent church (centre) was built in 1637–56 for the staff and students of the university. If it happens to be closed when you visit, you could enter Rundetårn and look down the church nave through the glass panel at the start of the ramp.

6 Vor Frue Kirke

In the 12th century, Bishop Absalon founded a Gothic church on this site. After burning down twice, the present Neo-Classical building (above and above left) was completed in 1829, but the tower is from medieval times. One of the bells is Denmark's oldest (1490) and another (weighing 4 tonnes) is the biggest.

7 Sankt Petri Kirke

Older than Vor Frue Kirke, this church also suffered from city fires and the British bombardment (1807). It has a vaulted sepulchral chapel with monuments and tombs that date back to 1681–83.

8 Regensen

Opposite the Rundetårn, this student residence was built in the 17th century. It burned down in the great fire of 1728, but was rebuilt not long after. Even today, the students retain several old traditions, including "storming" Rundetårn every May.

9 Højbro Plads

The equestrian statue (left) on this popular square depicts Bishop Absalon, founder of Copenhagen, pointing towards the site of his original castle on Slotsholmen.

10 Gråbrødretorv

Named after the Grey Brothers who built Copenhagen's first monastery here, this 13th-century square is now a popular place to eat in the open air.

The Bells and Carillion of Helligåndskirken

In 1647, 50 years after the clock tower was built, architect king Christian IV gifted the church a set of bells and a grand carillion. The carillion consisted of 19 bells and chimed a verse from a hymn every 30 minutes. It was also used at funerals; the importance of the deceased depended on the duration for which it played. This was at times taken too far, as playwright Ludwig Holberg (1684–1754) said when the carillion played for four straight hours: "A soul need not be so long on its way to heaven as the mail horse is to Roskilde". They were destroyed in the fire of 1728.

For more information on shops in the area and along nearby Strøget, see pp68–9.

🔟 Kongens Nytorv and Nyhavn

Kongens Nytorv (King's New Square) and Nyhavn (New Harbour) are two of the most picturesque areas in Copenhagen. It's hard to imagine the square was once outside the city gates and the site of the town gallows in medieval times. The Nyhavn canal was planned by Frederik III to connect the Inner Harbour with the square, enabling merchants to unload their goods more easily. The canal area is full of colourful houses and the bars and cafés come alive with visitors in summer. In winter, Kongens Nytorv becomes a popular skating rink.

Equestrian statue

🕐 The bars and restaurants on the south side of Nyhavn are usually not as busy as those on the north.

🍴 If you are looking for a quick bite away from the crowds, check out the Thomas Sandwich shop at 14 Lille Strandstræde.

• Map K4–L4
• Charlottenborg Slot: Nyhavn 2; 33 13 40 22; open noon–8pm Tue–Fri, noon–5pm Sat–Sun; adm 60kr, seniors and students 40kr; www.kunsthalcharlottenborg.dk
• Amber Museum: Kongens Nytorv 2; 33 11 67 00; open May–Sep 10am–6:30pm daily, Oct–Apr 10am–6pm daily; adm • Magasin du Nord: Kongens Nytorv 13; open 10am–7pm Mon–Sat (to 8pm Fri, to 5pm Sat); www.magasin.dk
• Det Kongelige Teater: Kongens Nytorv; 33 69 69 33; guided tours at 11am Sun, book at the box office; Adm 75kr; www.kglteater.dk

Top 10 Features

1. Nyhavn
2. Nyhavn Nos 20, 67 and 18
3. Equestrian Statue
4. Hotel d'Angleterre
5. Charlottenborg Slot
6. Det Kongelige Teater
7. Magasin du Nord
8. Vingårdsstræde 6
9. Store Strandestræde and Lille Strandstræde
10. Amber Museum

1 Nyhavn
Running down to the Inner Harbour, this canal is flanked by 18th-century houses that belonged to merchants. A large anchor, in honour of sailors who lost their lives in Word War II, marks the starting point of Nyhavn.

2 Nyhavn Nos 20, 67, 18
These brightly painted merchants' houses were built at the same time as the harbour. Fairy-tale writer HC Andersen lived in them. He wrote his first tale, *The Tinder Box* (1835), at No 20.

3 Equestrian Statue
This bronze statue in the middle of Kongens Nytorv commemorates Christian V (1646–99) who rebuilt the square in 1670 in Neo-Classical style. Sculpted by the Frenchman Lamoureux, it shows the king dressed as a Roman emperor.

4 Hotel d'Angleterre
This is Copenhagen's oldest hotel (1755), and one of the oldest in the world. It has played host to royalty and countless celebrities, including Karen Blixen, Winston Churchill, Grace Kelly and Madonna.

 For more sights associated with HC Andersen, see pp38–9.

Charlottenborg Slot
An early example of the Danish Baroque style, this palace *(right)* was built by Frederik III's legitimate son Ulrik in 1672–83. Today it houses the Royal Danish Academy of Fine Arts and Kunsthal Charlottenborg, a contemporary art museum. Walk along the north side of Nyhavn for a better view of the palace walls and to enter the courtyard.

Det Kongelige Teater
This Baroque-style theatre is the third one to stand on this site since 1749. It is home to the Royal Danish Theatre and the Royal Danish Ballet.

Vingårdsstræde 6
HC Andersen lived in this attic room for a year at the age of 22. You can enter the room from the third floor of the Magasin du Nord *(see right)*. No 6 is one of the oldest buildings in Copenhagen. Its 13th-century wine cellars (there used to be a vineyard here, hence *Vingårdsstræde*) now house a Michelin-starred restaurant.

Store Strandstræde and Lille Strandstræde
Once full of seedy pubs and brothels, "Big Beach Street" and "Little Beach Street" are now home to art galleries and stylish designer wear shops *(left)*. For a taste of its past, there are a couple of tattoo parlours down Store Strandstræde.

Amber Museum
Set in a house dating back to 1606, this museum *(right)* displays an exquisite collection dedicated to Denmark's national gem, amber (also called Nordic Gold). You will find amber antiques, pre-historic pieces and a 8.8-kg (19-lb) amber stone. Amber jewellery is also sold at the shop on the premises.

Magasin du Nord
Originally the famous Hotel du Nord, this Copenhagen's oldest department store *(left)* and is considered to be the city's answer to London's Selfridges or New York's Bloomingdale's. Standing to the north side of the Kongens Nytorv, the store will strike you as an impressive sight when you pass by. A range of restaurants are scattered throughout the building. Make sure you pay a visit to the Food Hall that is housed in the basement of the department store. The menu features a wide variety of delicious preparations that are worth sampling.

"The Imperial Ethiopian Palace" in Copenhagen
In the 1950s, Ethopia's Emperor Haile Selassie (also known as the King of Kings or the Conquering Lion of the Tribe of Judah), his wife and their entire family and entourage, visited Denmark's king and queen. In Copenhagen for only a few days, they stayed at the plush and luxurious Hotel d'Angleterre. A grand banquet was held in honour of Denmark's royal visitors in the Louis XVI Hall. During the time of their stay in the hotel, all telephone calls were answered with, "The Imperial Ethiopian Palace".

🔟 Amalienborg and Frederiksstaden

Built in the 1750s, this stately complex was designed by the royal architect, Nicolas Eigtved. Four Rococo palaces, originally home to four noble families, are set around an octagonal square in Frederiksstaden, an artistocratic area built by Frederik V. The king bought the palaces after the Christiansborg Palace burned down in 1794. The royal family has lived here ever since. It was named after a palace built on this site by Queen Sophie Amalie in the 17th century, which burned down in 1689 during a theatrical performance.

Amaliehaven

🍃 The guards will not respond well to people sitting on palace steps.

🍴 Head down Amaliegade to the bars and cafés along Nyhavn.

• Map L3
• Christian VII's Palace: 33 92 64 51; guided tours only Jul–Sep 1pm & 2:30pm in English; adm 75kr
• Christian VIII's Palace: 33 12 08 08; open Nov–Apr 11am–4pm Tue–Sun, May–Oct 10am–4pm daily; adm for adults 50kr, students 30kr, free with Copenhagen Card; www.ses.dk/amalienborg
• Marmorkirken: Frederiksgade 4; 33 15 01 44; open 10am–7pm Mon–Thu, noon–5pm Fri–Sun; www.marmorkirken.dk
• Frederik VIII's and Christian IX's palaces are not open to the public

Top 10 Features

1. Christian VII's Palace
2. Christian VIII's Palace
3. Frederik VIII's Palace
4. Christian IX's Palace
5. Equestrian Statue of Frederik V
6. Marmorkirken
7. Amaliehaven
8. Palace Guards
9. The Golden Axis
10. The Colonade

1 Christian VII's Palace

This palace was one of the first to be completed by the time of Eigtved's death in 1754. Also known as Moltke Palace, named after its original owner, Count Adam Gottlob Moltke, it is the most expensive palace in the complex and also has one of Denmark's best Rococo interiors. The queen often uses it to welcome foreign guests.

2 Christian VIII's Palace

This is where Crown Prince Frederik lived until his marriage to Australian Mary Donaldson in 2004. Part of the palace is open all year round as a museum that is dedicated to the Glücksberg Dynasty. Visit Queen Louise's chintzy drawing room and the studies of several kings.

Marmorkirken

3 Frederik VIII's Palace

Previously known as Brockdorff's Palace, this palace *(left)* with a clock on its façade was renamed after Frederik VIII moved into it in 1869. More recently, it was home to Queen Dowager Ingrid (Queen Margrethe's mother) till her death in 2000. Since 2010 it has been the residence of Crown Prince Frederik and Crown Princess Mary.

4 Christian IX's Palace

The first royal family to live here was Crown Prince Frederik IV and his wife (1794). Since 1967, it has been home to Queen Margrethe and Prince Consort Henrik.

5 Equestrian Statue of Frederik V

Designed and cast (1753–71) by French sculptor Jacques Saly, this statue of Frederik V is said to have cost four times as much as Amalienborg. Saly, who stayed here for 18 years, was known for the extravagant parties he hosted. His expenses were paid by the Danish Asiatic Company, who gifted this statue to the king.

6 Marmorkirken

Properly called Frederikskirken, the Marble Church *(left)* got its popular name on account of plans to build it using Norwegian marble. Its dome, one of the largest in Europe and modelled after St Peter's in Rome, has a diameter of 31 m (102 ft).

7 Amaliehaven

The Amalie Garden was created in 1993 on the banks of the Harbour, financed by the shipping giant AP Møller and the Christine McKinney Møller Foundation. It has a splendid fountain that lies on Copenhagen's "Golden Axis" *(see below),* between the Opera House and the statue of Frederik V.

8 Palace Guards

When the queen is in residence, the Danish Royal Life Guards *(right)* stand outside the palace, guarding their monarch in 2-hour shifts. At noon they are replaced by the guards from Rosenborg Castle *(see pp14–15),* who march through the streets of Copenhagen every day at 11:30am to switch places with the guards at Amalienborg Palace.

The Russian Connection

A stone's throw from Marmorkirken, the golden onion domes of Alexander Nevsky Kirke, the Russian Orthodox Cathedral, are easily identifiable *(see p78).* Consecrated in 1883, it was a gift from the future Tsar Alexander III to mark his marriage to the Danish Princess Marie Dagmar in St Petersburg in 1866. It was in this church that her funeral was held when she passed away in 1928.

9 The Golden Axis

The Marble Church and Frederiksstaden lie on short axis called the Golden Axis. This axis was considered so important that when the Opera House was built along this line, it caused much controversy. The building is now considered the axis' modern extension.

0 The Colonnade

This Classical-style colonnade was built by Christian VII's royal architect, Caspar Frederik Harsdorff in 1794–95. Supported by eight ionic columns, it runs unobtrusively from one palace to another along the first-floor level.

🔟 Statens Museum for Kunst

Denmark's national gallery is housed in two buildings – one dating back to the 19th century and the other, a stylish, modern extension, linked by a bridge over a sculpture gallery known as Sculpture Street. The museum's collections span international and national paintings, sculptures, installations, prints and drawings from the 14th century to the present. The national collection specialises in paintings from the Golden Age and by later 19th-century artists such as the Skagen school, the rebels of their time.

The modern extension

⭐ The children's museum provides activities every Saturday and Sunday through the summer holidays.

The department of prints and drawings has fascinating works dating back to the 15th century, including those by Rembrandt, Manet and Picasso.

⭐ The bright, stylish museum café looks out onto Ostre Anlæg Lake. In good weather, the park is ideal for a picnic.

• Map J2
• Sølvgade 48–50
• 33 74 84 94
• Open 10am–5pm Tue–Sun, 10am–8pm Wed, Closed Mon
• Guided tours for families are also available
• Free except for special exhibitions; Copenhagen Card accepted (see p111)
• smk@smk.dk
• www.smk.dk

Top 10 Features

1. Sculpture Street
2. Christ as the Suffering Redeemer
3. The X-Room
4. Portrait of Bellini
5. The Judgement of Solomon
6. Boys Bathing in Skagen
7. Portrait of Madame Matisse
8. Alice
9. The Wheel of Life
10. The Earth Weeps

The X-Room
Experimental space with changing installations by young international artists. The black box interior is transformed into fantastic, multimedia worlds.

Sculpture Street
This impressive, varied collection of sculptures runs the entire length of the building. The displays look resplendent beneath the sunlight streaming in through the glass roof. Don't miss Sørensen's extraordinary display of ferocious dogs.

Christ as the Suffering Redeemer
This striking painting (1495–1500) by prominent Renaissance artist Andrea Mantegna shows the Resurrection of Christ on the third day after his crucifixion. Mantegna known for his profound interest ancient Roman civilization; in th painting *(left)*, it comes through with the porphyry sarcophagus.

Portrait of the Venetian painter Giovanni Bellini

This portrait of Giovanni Bellini, official painter for the Venetian Republic, is an early work (1511–12) by the Venetian artist Tiziano Vecellio (better known as Titian).

The Judgement of Solomon

This painting by Rubens depicts the inspiring story from the Old Testament, where the wisdom of King Solomon is tested. The interplay of colours is an important part of the drama. Though created by Rubens, much of the brushwork was done by assistants.

Boys Bathing in Skagen, Summer Evening

This intriguing painting (left) by Peder S. Krøyer (see p35) shows three little boys playing on the beach in the moonlight. It was submitted to the World Exhibition held in Paris in 1900.

Key

- Ground floor
- First floor
- Second floor

Portrait of Madame Matisse

Also known as The Green Stripe, this painting by Henri Matisse of his wife was to have far-reaching repercussions in the art world. It was one of several radical paintings in the 1905 Salon d'Automne and helped give rise to the Fauvist movement known for its bright colours and spontaneous style.

Alice

One of over 300 portraits by Amedeo Modigliani painted between 1915 and 1920, this beautiful painting reflects the artist's interest in African sculpture. He has made use of simple shapes and stylised features to create an idealised portrait.

The Wheel of Life

Belonging to the Suite of Seasons series, this painting (1953) by Asger Jorn (see p35) represents the month of January. Alluding to the medieval concept of "the wheel of life", Jorn, who was suffering from tuberculosis, was inspired to paint this in the hope for better health.

The Earth Weeps

This powerful painting (1981) by award-winning Danish painter, Svend Wiig Hansen, reflects the artist's early life amidst widespread violence, fear and misery, especially during the Spanish Civil War and World War II. The theme of violence is a constant feature in most of his work.

Museum Guide

Situated within the public park of Østre Anlæg, visitors can enter the museum from the corner of Sølvgade and Øster Voldgade. The lobby is flanked by temporary exhibitions and a bookshop. The ground floor is taken up by Sculpture Street and the X-Room, with international art in the extension on the first floor. The old main building houses modern Danish art.

🔟 Ny Carlsberg Glyptotek

This marvellous glyptotek (which means "a collection of statues") is set inside two 19th-century buildings linked by a charming Winter Garden and a modern wing designed by architect Henning Larsen. It contains the world-class collections of Carl Jacobsen (see p84) and his son Helge, as well as some recent additions. Exhibits range from ancient Egyptian, Greek and Roman sculpture, to early 19th- and 20th-century Danish and French art. The roof terrace affords great views of the city and Tivoli Gardens.

Dahlerup building façade

🚶 Guided tours in English are held in the summer at 2pm on Wednesdays and in Danish on Sundays. Free tickets are available at the ticket counter; no advance booking.

🍴 The Winter Garden has a pleasant café, which isn't too expensive. Otherwise, you can picnic discreetly on the roof terrace of the new wing.

- Map H6
- Dantes Plads 7
- 33 41 81 41
- Open 11am–5pm Tue–Sun
- Adm for adults 60kr, free on Sun, under 18 years free; Copenhagen Card accepted (see p111)
- info@glyptoteket.dk
- www.glyptoteket.dk

Top 10 Features

1. The Ancient Mediterranean Collection
2. The Greek Collection
3. The Roman Collection
4. The Egyptian Collection
5. Danish Golden Age Paintings
6. The French Impressionists
7. The Post-Impressionists
8. 19th-century Danish Sculpture
9. 19th-century French Sculpture
10. The Winter Garden

Key

- ▨ Ground floor
- ▨ First floor
- ▨ Second floor

1 The Ancient Mediterranean Collection

Located in the new wing of the museum, this collection has fascinating artifacts, particularly from the Middle East and Etruria. The most impressive pieces are the Etruscan sarcophagi dating back to the period between 200–150 BC.

2 The Greek Collection

The collection *(left)* has works of art from the 6th–1st centuries BC. A highlight is one of the earliest Attic healing-god reliefs (around 420 BC), which depicts a daughter of Hygeia, god of healing, promising health to Athenians during a plague. There is also a rare and beautiful marble portrait bust of Alexander the Great.

3 The Roman Collection

There are some excellent busts of Rome's public figures in this collection, including those of luminaries such as General Pompey, Emperor Augustus, the evil and depraved Caligula and Emperor Hadrian, considered to be one of the best rulers of the empire.

The Egyptian Collection
Much of this collection is displayed in underground chambers into which you descend, as if in a mummy's tomb. There are also some huge sculptures *(left)*, like that of the god Ptah with King Ramesses II (1290–1224 BC). The oldest piece is a small, 5,000-year old hippo.

Danish Golden Age Paintings
Here you will find great works of art from Denmark's Golden Age (1800–50), a period when art and culture blossomed despite political and economic strife. The greatest artists of the period, Eckersberg, Købke and Lundbye are especially well represented.

The French Impressionists
This collection includes paintings by Manet, Renoir, Sisley, Monet and Pissarro, among a host of other artists. The *Absinthe Drinker* by Manet is a particular highlight, as is the remarkable Degas bronze ballerina *(right)*.

The Post-Impressionists
This splendid gallery holds early works of artists like Van Gogh *(right)* and Cézanne, as well as the world's largest collection of Gauguin paintings.

19th-century Danish Sculpture
Includes works by Denmark's Neo-Classical sculptors, like Villhelm Bissen and Jens Jerichau. Bissen's *Danaid* (1880), epitomises Neo-Classical style.

19th-century French Sculpture
This stunning collection features the biggest names in French sculpture, including Rodin, Barye, Maillol Carpeaux, Dubois and Falguière.

The Winter Garden
This glass-domed garden is a great place relax amid statues, including a replica of *The Water Mother* (1921), by Danish sculptor Kai Nielsen.

Museum Guide

Enter the museum from HC Andersens Boulevard. Buy tickets downstairs and walk straight ahead to the Winter Garden. On the left is the entrance to the Larsen building and the French Impressionist collection. Walk through the Winter Garden and up a few steps to the grand Central Hall, with its collection of Greek, Roman and Egyptian antiquities. The 19th-century Danish and French art collections are on this floor as well as on the second floor.

⟲10 Nationalmuseet

Denmark's largest museum, the National Museum, presents the history and culture of the Danes from prehistoric times to the present. It also houses a wonderful collection of Greek and Egyptian antiquities, an ethnographic collection and the Children's Museum. Many of the displays derive from King Frederik III's Royal Cabinet of Curiosities put together around 1650. The state collection has had several homes and is housed in the 18th-century Rococo Prince's Palace at Frederiksholms Kanal, where it has been since the 1850s.

The museum atrium

🍃 **The Victorian Home,** a plush apartment with authentic 19th-century interiors, owned by the museum, is also located nearby.

🍴 Visit the museum café on the second floor, or go to Ny Carlsberg Glyptotek *(see pp24–5),* for lunch in the delightful Winter Garden.

• Map J5
• Ny Vestergade 10
• 33 13 44 11
• Open 10am–5pm Tue–Sun • Free
• Free guided tours in English, Jun–Sep 11am every Tue, Thu and Sun
• Call for details of activities in the Children's Museum
• Guided tours of the Victorian Home in English: Jun–Sep 2pm every Sat (tickets are available from the information desk in the National Museum lobby); adm for adults 50kr, concessions 40kr, free for under-18s
• www.natmus.dk

Top 10 Features

1 The Sun Chariot
2 Oak Burial Coffins
3 Gundestrup Cauldron
4 State Rooms
5 Inuit Culture
6 China, Japan and the Far East
7 Prehistoric Denmark and the Viking Age
8 Room 117
9 Cylinder Perspective Table
10 Denmark's Oldest Coin

Key

▨ Ground floor
▨ First floor
▨ Second floor
▨ Third floor

The Sun Chariot
The unique Sun Chariot or *Solvognen (right),* a masterpiece of casting, was dug up in 1902 by a farmer ploughing his field. This 3,400-year-old artifact from the Bronze Age shows a horse on wheels pulling a large sun disk, gilded only on one side to represent its daytime trajectory.

Oak Burial Coffins
Seven oak, Bronze-Age coffins, dating back to 1,400 BC, occupy space on the ground floor. The Egtved grave, holding the body of a well-preserved, fully clad young woman is an extraordinary exhibit.

Gundestrup Cauldron
Found near Gundestrup, this silver cauldron *(right)* from the Iron Age, is decorated with animals and mystical figures.

State Rooms
The State Rooms date back to the time when this building was a royal palace. They are virtually intact from the period 1743–44; the Great Hall is adorned with the original Flemish tapestries to this day.

5 Inuit Culture

This collection *(left)* from Greenland showcases the skill and creative ingenuity from the frozen North. The displays include boats and clothing like embroidered anoraks and boots, assorted toys and watercolours of daily life.

6 China, Japan and the Far East

The Far East is well represented in this marvellous collection that includes Japanese laquerwork, fabulously costumed Samurai warriors, replete with weaponry and beautiful 18th-century Imperial Dragon robes, worn by the Chinese emperor.

7 Prehistoric Denmark and the Viking Age

The museum's most popular exhibit is this comprehensive display of the country's 14,000-year history. These intricate golden horns *(right)*, reconstructed in the 20th century after the 400 BC originals were melted down in 1802, are a definite highlight.

8 Room 117

This 18th-century bourgeois interior can be traced to the town of Aalborg in Jutland. A wood-panelled room in a sea of glass-display galleries, it features a heavy wooden four-poster bed, chest, coffered wooden ceiling and mullioned windows.

9 Cylinder Perspective Table

In Room 126, this table is a part of Frederik III's Royal Cabinet of Curiosities. The table top shows him and his wife, Sophie Amalie, painted ingeniously in a distorted perspective: it gets rectified when viewed in the reflective surface of a cylinder at the centre of the table.

10 Denmark's Oldest Coin

The name of Denmark and an image of a Danish king were first depicted on this small silver coin *(left)* – found in Room 144 – that was struck in AD 995.

Museum Guide

Fronted by a courtyard, the museum's entrance hall has lavatories and lockers. You can pick up a map and information in the atrium straight ahead. The museum shop, also located here, sells some interesting books and educational toys with a Viking twist. The Children's Museum is to your left. If you are time-bound, opt for the one-hour themed itineraries. The prehistoric collection is on the ground floor, while the first floor holds a range of collections, including one on ethnography. The second floor includes a history of Denmark collection (from 1660 to 2000). The antiquities are found on the third floor.

Slotsholmen

The small fishing village of Copenhagen was founded on the island of Slotsholmen in the 12th century. Bishop Absalon, the king's friend and supporter, built a castle here in 1167. Two centuries later, the castle was destroyed by the Hanseatic League, the European trade alliance that resented Copenhagen's increasing control over trade. Christiansborg Palace, which stands here today, is home to the Danish Parliament, the Jewish Museum and the Palace Church.

Teatermuseet
This delightful court theatre, above the Royal Stables, was established in 1767. Now a museum, it depicts Danish theatre in the 18th and 19th centuries. The atmosphere is enhanced by classical music and displays of mannequins in court dresses. Visitors can also walk onto the stage.

Christiansborg Slotskirke

🍽 **Visit the restaurants on Gammel Strand and Højbro Plads.**

- Map J5
- Christiansborg Slot: 33 92 64 92; open May–Sep 10am–4pm daily; Oct–Apr Tue–Sun 10am–4pm; guided tours of State Rooms May–Sep 3pm daily; Oct–Apr 3pm Tue–Sun; adm; www. christiansborgpalace.dk
- Ruins: open May–Sep 10am–4pm daily; Oct–Apr 10am–4pm Tue–Sun; adm
- Royal Stables: 33 40 26 76; open 2–4pm Sat–Sun (also May–Sep 2–4pm Fri); adm
- Royal Library Gardens: open all year
- Christiansborg Slotskirke: open noon–4pm Sun; Jul: daily • Tøjhusmuseet: 33 11 60 37; open noon–4pm Tue–Sun; weeks 7, 8, 42 & Jul 10am–4pm daily; adm; www.thm.dk
- Thorvaldsens Museum: Bertel Thorvaldsens Plads 2; 33 32 15 32; open 10am–5pm Tue–Sun; adm

Top 10 Features

1. Christiansborg Slot
2. Ruins Under the Palace
3. Teatermuseet
4. The Royal Stables
5. Royal Library Gardens
6. Tøjhusmuseet
7. Dansk Jødisk Museum
8. Christiansborg Slotskirke
9. Thorvaldsens Museum
10. The Royal Reception Rooms

Christiansborg Slot
Designed in a Neo-Baroque style in 1907–28 *(right)*, this sturdy construction is built from reinforced concrete and granite-lined façades. It houses the state rooms, the Folketinget (the elected parliament), the Prime Minister's apartment and the High Court. The 106-m (350-ft) high tower is the tallest one in the city.

Ruins Under The Palace
These fascinating ruins were discovered during the construction of the present palace. You can see parts of Bishop Absalon's castle *(see p65)* and the second castle that stood here until the 18th century. You will also find interesting details of the routine of daily life, such as a baker's oven, latrine chutes and hollow tree trunks used as underground pipes.

The Royal Stables
The stables *(below)* of Christian VI's Palace survived the fire of 1794. The queen's horses are still kept here amid splendid marble walls, columns and mangers. There is also a collection of royal coaches and riding gear.

The Ruins, Tøjhusmuseet and Thorvaldsens Museum all accept the Copenhagen Card, see p111.

5 The Royal Library Gardens

Formerly a naval port, this oasis is tucked behind Christiansborg (right). Designed in 1920, the fountains in the central pool cascade every hour. Check out the statue of philosopher Kierkegaard.

6 Tøjhusmuseet

Built as an arsenal by Christian IV in 1604–08, the Royal Danish Arsenal Museum is filled with artillery guns. The Armoury Hall on the first floor has 7,000 hand weapons, some from the 1300s.

9 Thorvaldsens Museum

This orange-walled museum is home to almost all of Bertel Thorvaldsen's works and some of his personal belongings. In the entrance hall are the original plaster casts of some of his most famous pieces. In 1848, his tomb was moved to the museum's courtyard.

10 The Royal Reception Rooms

Christiansborg's state rooms are used by Denmark's Royal Family for official functions. Enter the rooms via the Queen's Gate, the Guard's Room and the King's Stairway. Note the Throne Room, with its huge ceiling painting, and the Great Hall with 17 royal tapestries, which recount the history of Denmark and were presented to the Queen by Bjørn Nørgaard (see p35).

Castle Island

Several castles have stood on this site through the centuries. The first one was built in 1167 by Bishop Absalon. A second castle, occupied by the king, Eric of Pomerania, was built in 1417. When the building was beginning to fall apart, it was demolished in 1731 by Christian VI. In its place, he built a Baroque palace he considered suitable for an Absolute Monarch. It was completed in 1745, but was destroyed in the fire of 1794. Another castle was built in 1803–28, but also burned down in 1884. Finally, the present castle was built in 1907–28.

7 Dansk Jødisk Museum

This museum (below) has a striking modern interior, designed by architect Daniel Libeskind. The small building brilliantly depicts the lives and culture of the Jewish population in Denmark.

8 Christiansborg Slotskirke

Standing on the site of the original 18th-century palace church destroyed in the infamous fire of 1794, this Neo-Classical church with warm, yellow walls was built in 1813–26. However, a fire broke out in 1992 and destroyed its roof, dome and even parts of the interior. A service is held here every October for the opening of Parliament (see also p41).

For full details and opening times for Teatermuseet and the Dansk Jødisk Museum, see pp34–5.

Detail from a painting showing the destruction of the Danish navy, 1801

Moments in History

1 The Founding of Copenhagen

Copenhagen was founded around AD 1000 on the island of Slotsholmen *(see pp28–9)* by Sweyn I Forkbeard, son of Harald Bluetooth. Forkbeard was the first Danish king to strike coins with his image upon them. He subjugated Denmark, Norway and England, which he ruled for five weeks before his death in 1014.

2 The Growth of Trade

Given by Valdemar I to his adviser, Bishop Absalon, in the 1160s, the fishing village of Havn (harbour) prospered greatly from the shoals of herring that appeared in its waters. A castle was built here as protection against raiders. The prosperity of Havn became a threat to the Hanseatic league, an alliance of trading guilds that monopolized trade in Northern Europe. They repeatedly attacked the castle, finally destroying it in 1367.

Søren Kierkegaard

3 Copenhagen, Capital of Denmark

King Erik VII took up residence in the second castle in 1416 and by this time Havn, now Kjøbmande-havn (Merchants' Harbour), was a major economic centre. It was proclaimed as the capital of Denmark in 1443.

4 Civil War and the Reformation

Between 1534 and 1536, the Protestant king, Christian III successfully withstood an uprising against him in favour of his Catholic cousin, Christian II. Christian III brought about the Reform-ation in Denmark.

5 Absolute Monarchy

In 1660, Frederik III introduced Absolute Monarchy, enhanc-ing the powers of the middle classes. Frederik VII later abolished it in favour of an elected Parliament.

6 Wars with Sweden

Sharing the Sound meant the Swedes and Danes were in constant dispute. In the winter of 1657, the Swedes crossed the frozen Sound on foot, attac-king Copenhagen. The ensuing Treaty of Roskilde saw Denmark cede its Swedish territories.

Bombardment of Copenhagen, 1807

  Preceding pages: **Ceiling of the Marmorkirken dome.**

Ceremony introducing Absolute Monarchy

7 The Great Plague
Between June 1711 and March 1712, Copenhagen was hit by bubonic plague, wiping out 20,000 of its 60,000 inhabitants. It is said to have been brought in by ships from Sweden or East Prussia, carrying infected vermin.

8 The Fire of 1728
In the month of October, within four days, the greatest fire in Copenhagen's history wiped out almost all of northern Copenhagen. It began early in the morning at Vester Kvarter 146 – now roughly at the top of Strøget. Five churches, the university library, and 1,600 houses were destroyed.

9 The Battles of Copenhagen
Early in the 19th century, the city suffered more lasting damage when the British attacked in 1801, destroying the Danish navy, and again in 1807 to discourage the Danes from supporting France in the Napoleonic wars.

10 Rescue of the Danish Jews
The Nazis occupied Denmark during World War II from 1940–45. In 1943, when the Jews were ordered to be deported to Germany, a collective of Danes and Swedes secretly evacuated virtually the entire Jewish population to Sweden by sea. As a result, most Danish Jews survived the war.

Top 10 Historical Figures

1 Harald Bluetooth (911–987)
He converted Denmark to Christianity.

2 King Cnut (994/5–1035)
Ruled England, Norway and Denmark for 20 years and famously failed to hold back the waves.

3 Bishop Absalon (1128–1201)
A warrior bishop, he built the first castle on Slotsholmen.

4 Christian IV (1577–1648)
He promoted shipping and trade and built the Rundetårn and Rosenborg Palace.

5 Tycho Brahe (1546–1601)
Brahe's astronomical tables were used to plot the rules of planetary motion.

6 Vitus Jonasson Bering (1681–1741)
A Danish explorer who discovered the Bering Strait, Sea, Island and Land Bridge.

7 Hans Christian Ørsted (1777–1851)
Danish physicist who discovered electromagnetism.

8 Søren Kierkegaard (1813–55)
A Danish philosopher, who first put forward the theory of "existentialism".

9 Knud Rasmussen (1879–1933)
He was the first man to cross the Northwest Passage by dogsled.

10 Niels Bohr (1885–1962)
A Nobel prize-winner (1922), he contributed vastly to the understanding of quantum mechanics.

Left **Teatermuseet** Centre **Kunstindustrimuseet** Right **Thorvaldsens Museum**

🔟 Museums and Galleries

1 Ny Carlsberg Glyptotek

The museum houses a fabulous collection of antiquities from Egypt, Greece, Rome and the Mediterranean coast. You will also find an impressive collection of 19th- and early 20th-century Danish and French fine arts, including Impressionist and Post-Impressionist collections *(see pp24–5)*.

Egyptian statues at Ny Carlsberg Glyptotek

2 Nationalmuseet

This is Denmark's largest museum of cultural history. Here you can explore the history of the Danes right up to the present day. Artifacts range from Iron Age burials and Renaissance interiors to African masks and houses on stilts. Check out the museum's spectacular ethnographic collection including the world's oldest painting by South American Indians *(see pp26–7)*.

Viking culture at the Nationalmuseet

3 Statens Museum for Kunst

Nestled in a park with lakes and grassy slopes, the National Gallery displays a large collection of international art, with works by Great Masters like Dürer and Titian and by modern icons such as Picasso and Matisse. These are displayed side by side with 20th-century Danish works, including those of the controversial CoBrA group *(see pp22–3)*.

4 Dansk Jødisk Museum

The Danish Jewish Museum tells the story of Denmark's Jewish community since the arrival of the first families in the 17th century. Designed by architect Daniel Libeskind, the interlocking interior symbolises Danish-Jewish good relations, its apogee the rescue of 7,000 Jews from Nazis. ◎ *Map K5 • Proviantpassangen 6 • 33 11 22 18 • Open Sep–May 1pm–4pm Tue–Fri, noon–5pm Sat–Sun; Jun–Aug 10am–5pm Tue–Sun • Adm for adults; free with Copenhagen Card • www.jewmus.dk*

5 Davids Samling

Set inside a 19th-century town house, the museum holds the collections of Christian Ludwig David (1878–1960), a Danish barrister. It includes fabulous furniture from the 18th–20th centuries and ancient Islamic ornamental art *(see p76)*.

*For more museums and galleries, see **pp19, 28–9, 56–7, 64–6, 78, 82–5, 90.***

6 Teatermuseet

On display are sections including the stage, the auditorium and dressing rooms of the 18th-century Royal Theatre *(see p19)* that survived the fire of 1794.
• Map J5 • Christiansborg Ridebane 18 • 33 11 51 76 • Open 11am–3pm Tue & Thu, 11am–5pm Wed, 1–4pm Sat–Sun • Adm for adults; free with Copenhagen Card • www.teatermuseet.dk

7 Frihedsmuseet

The Danish Resistance Museum is part of the national collection. It takes you through a fascinating exploration of Danish life during the Nazi occupation from 1940–45 *(see p77).*

8 Kunstindustrimuseet

One half of the Danish Museum of Decorative Art holds a collection of Chinese and Japanese artifacts, as well as European medieval and Rococo arts. The other half is dedicated to cutting-edge Danish 20th- and 21st-century design. English labelling is limited *(see p77).*

9 Thorvaldsens Museum

Opened in 1848, this museum pays homage to the Neo-Classical sculptor, Bertel Thorvaldsen. It includes most of his works, as well as some private belongings. You can also visit his grave, transferred here from Vor Frue Kirke in 1848, four years after his demise *(see p28).*

10 Den Hirschsprungske Samling

Housed in a villa, across the lake from the Statens Museum for Kunst, it features a collection of late 19th- and early 20th-century Danish art – notably the Skagen school, Denmark's equally appealing answer to the Impressionists *(see p75).*

Top 10 Danish Artists

1 Bertel Thorvaldsen (1770–1844)
Son of an Icelandic wood carver, he became Denmark's most famous sculptor.

2 Christoffer Eckersberg (1783–1853)
Laid the foundations for the "Golden Age of Painting" in Denmark (1800–1850).

3 Michael Ancher (1849–1927)
One of the best-known artists in Denmark and the unofficial head of the Skagen group.

4 Peder Severin Krøyer (1851–1909)
His work is inspired by the lives of the fishermen of Skagen.

5 Anna Ancher (1859–1935)
A Skagen artist and wife of Michael Ancher. Her work is typified by picturesque, intimate scenes of family life.

6 Vilhelm Hammershøi (1864–1916)
Known for his paintings of interiors, done in muted colours.

7 Richard Mortensen (1910–1993)
The first Danish artist to turn to abstraction. Also known for his perfect technical finish.

8 Carl-Henning Pedersen (1913–2007)
An expressionist surrealist and one of the most influential artists of the CoBrA group.

9 Asger Jorn (1914–73)
Founder of CoBrA, an important art group to emerge after World War II.

10 Bjørn Nørgaard (1947–)
One of the most influential Danish contemporary artists, his works span a range of fields, including sculpture. He also designed the Queen's Tapestries.

For museums and galleries out of town, see pp96–102.

Left **Rosenborg Slot** Centre **Den Sorte Diamant** Right **Christiansborg Slot**

🔟 Historic Buildings

1 Rosenborg Slot
This lovely, turreted Renaissance castle was built by Christian IV. Now a royal museum, its collections and interior provide a vivid picture of the monarchy over the centuries. The crown jewels are on display in the basement *(see pp14–15)*.

2 Christiansborg Slot
This Neo-Baroque palace, built in the early 20th century, is the seat of the government and the fourth palace on the site. Visit the 12th–14th-century ruins of the first two castles built here, the 18th-century theatre and stables and the state rooms *(see p28)*.

3 Rundetårn
This curious Round Tower was built by Christian IV and affords a wonderful view over the old town. It also has a gallery that holds innovative, changing exhibitions *(see p16)*.

4 Børsen
The stock exchange is remarkable for its tower with a striking spire designed to look like four entwined dragons' tails. The three crowns at the top of the building represent the kingdoms of Denmark, Sweden and Norway. ◈ Map K5
• Børsgade • Not open to the public

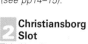

Chapel Portal at Frederiksborg Slot

5 Frederiksborg Slot
This beautiful, grand Renaissance castle is a short train ride away from Copenhagen. Christian IV was living here when he fell seriously ill and demanded to be taken to his favourite palace, Rosenborg, for his last few days. Don't miss the castle's ornate chapel *(see p98)*.

6 Regensen
Built by Christian IV in the 17th century as a student hostel, Regensen still retains that function today. Unfortunately, most of the building was burnt down in the city fire of 1728 *(see p33)*, but so vital was it to the life of the university that it was rebuilt shortly after *(see p17)*.

7 Radisson Blu Royal Hotel
A 1960s icon or a horrible tower block? Designed by architect Arne Jacobsen *(see p39)*, this hotel underwent a makeover in the 1980s; the original interior was retained only in Room 606. If it is unoccupied and you ask nicely, they might let you have a look at the room. The foyer has a 1960s retro cool look and includes Jacobsen's interesting Swan and Egg chairs. You can enjoy excellent views of the city from the restaurant *(see also p83)*.

8 Holmens Kirke

The only Renaissance church in Copenhagen, it was originally built as a sailors' forge in 1562–63 and converted into a naval church by Christian IV in 1619. The strangely exotic font is the work of a local 17th-century blacksmith. The metal fence shows golden elephants carrying black castles on their backs, a depiction of the royal Danish elephant. ◈ *Map K5 • Holmens Kanal • 33 13 61 78 • Open 9am–2pm Mon–Sat*

9 Den Sorte Diamant

The Black Diamond, a modern extension of the Royal Library, was built by architects Schmidt, Hammer and Lassen. It houses the National Museum of Photography, the Queen's Hall concert space, an exhibition area and Søren K, a smart restaurant. The shiny tiled exterior is highly reflective and a favourite photo opportunity for the boat trippers floating past *(see p8)*.

10 Operaen

The remarkable Opera House stands on the banks of the Holmen, formerly Copenhagen's naval dockyard. The auditorium is a masterpiece of acoustic design, from the velour seats that do not absorb sound, to the distance between the front of the stage and the back wall, which allows for the perfect time to achieve greater clarity for opera. Over 100,000 pieces of 23.75 carat gold leaves make up the ceiling *(see p8)*.

Operaen

Top 10 Statues

1 Little Mermaid
The city's icon, inspired by the fairy tale. ◈ *Langelinie, top end of Kastellet*

2 Gefionspringvandet
Statue depicting the fable of goddess Gefion and the king of Denmark. ◈ *Langelinie, by St Alban's Church*

3 Fiskerkone
The Fishwife was created in 1940 and installed at the spot where fish have been sold since the medieval times. ◈ *Gammel Strand*

4 Lurblæserne
It is said that the Hornblowers will sound the Viking horns whenever a virgin passes by – no one has heard a peep out of them yet. ◈ *Rådhuspladsen*

5 Frederik V
Sculptor Jacques Saly took 20 years to finish this statue. Unveiled in 1771, it merited a 27-gun salute. ◈ *Amalienborg Slotsplads*

6 Christian V
Shows the king dressed as a Roman emperor riding over a fallen figure. ◈ *Kongens Nytorv*

7 Hans Christian Andersen
Famous sculpture by Henry Lukow-Nielsen. ◈ *Corner of Rådhus, HC Andersen Boulevard*

8 Hans Christian Andersen
Includes scenes from his fairy tales. ◈ *Kongens Have*

9 Caritas Springvandet
One of the oldest statues in Copenhagen, dating back to 1608. ◈ *Gammel Torv*

10 The Elephant Gate
Big, splendid elephants at the Carlsberg Brewery gateway. ◈ *Gammel Carlsberg Vej 11*

At the end of university exams in the Spring, it is traditional for Copenhagen's students to dance around the statue of Christian V.

Left **Vor Frue Kirke** Centre **Hotel d'Angleterre** Right **Nyhavn**

Hans Christian Andersen Sights

Det Kongelige Teater
Hans Christian Andersen arrived in Copenhagen on 6 September 1819 as a starstruck 14-year-old. It was "my second birthday", he recounts in his biography, *The Fairytale of My Life*. Determined to become an actor, he went straight to the Royal Theatre in search of a job. Although occasionally employed as an actor, his acting talent never quite matched his skill as a writer *(see p18)*.

Bakkehusmuseet
The Bakkehus (House on the Hill) was the home of prominent literary patron Knud Rahbek and his wife Kamma Lyhne Rahbek from 1802–1830. Andersen met the couple in the early 1820s and their home soon became a meeting place for poets and authors. The museum retains a homely atmosphere and recreates the Golden Age of creativity. It also includes various mementos that belonged to Andersen *(see pp84–5)*.

Vingårdsstræde 6
Andersen lived here for a year in 1827 in a spartan garret room (then No 132), preparing for his university exams. This is where he wrote the sad poem, *The Student*. The museum's entrance is on the third floor of the Magasin du Nord *(see p19)*.

Nyhavn Nos 20, 67 and 18
Andersen lived in lodgings in Nyhavn for much of his life, including at Nyhavn 280 (now No 20) in 1834, No 67 in 1848 and No 18 (a private hotel) in 1871. He lived here until 1875, when he fell terminally ill and moved in with the Melchiors, who nursed him in their own home *(see p18)*.

Magasin du Nord
In 1838, Andersen moved into Hotel du Nord, now the department store Magasin du Nord. Here he rented two rooms in the attic, one of which overlooked the Royal Theatre. Mini's Café (now Café à Porta) was next door and became a regular haunt for the writer *(see p18)*.

Rundetårn
The exhibition space here was once the university library where Andersen spent many hours. His first fairytale, *The Tinderbox* (1835), talks of a dog with eyes "as big as a tower" guarding a

Department store, Magasin (once Hotel) du Nord

See also the Wonderful World of HC Andersen Museum on **pp56, 66** and the Bakkehusmuseet on **p84**.

Rundetårn's cobbled spiral ramp

treasure. Scholars believe this refers to the Rundetårn, which was built as an observatory – a literal eye to the sky *(see p16)*.

7 Hotel d'Angleterre
Andersen stayed here in November 1860, when he occupied two rooms at the corner of Kongens Nytorv and Østergade (Strøget), close to the Royal Theatre; between August 1869 and March 1870; and finally, during April–May 1871 *(see p112)*.

8 Lille Kongensgade 1
In October 1866, Andersen took a suite of rooms on the third floor, rented out by a photographer, Thora Hallager. Here, he bought furniture for the first time in his life (at the age of 61), as this was an unfurnished apartment. 🔍 *Map K4*

9 Vor Frue Kirke
Andersen died on 4 August 1875 of liver cancer. His funeral, a national event attended by the king and crown prince, was held at Vor Frue Kirke in the Old Town *(see p17)*.

10 Assistens Kirkegård
This is the cemetery where Andersen's body was interred in Nørrebro. The stone is inscribed with inspirational lines from his poem "Oldingen" or "The Old Man" (1874) *(see p75)*.

Top 10 Danish Cultural Figures

1 August Bournonville (1805–1879)
Choreographer and ballet master who created many works for the Danish ballet.

2 Carl Nielsen (1865–1931)
Composer, violinist and pianist. Best known for his symphonies and the operas *Saul og David* and *Maskerade*.

3 Karen Blixen (1885–1962)
Her famous novel, *Out of Africa (1937)*, was published under the pen name Isak Dinesen.

4 Poul Henningsen (1894–1967)
Architect, author and anti-traditionalist. Best known for his PH lamps *(see p47)*.

5 Arne Jacobsen (1902–1971)
Architect and designer who defined the concept of Danish design – fluid and practical.

6 Lars von Trier (1956–)
Film director famous for the Dogme95 Collective and his technique of cinematic minimalism.

7 Peter Høeg (1957–)
Gained international acclaim for his story *Miss Smilla's Feeling for Snow* (1992).

8 Viggo Mortensen (1958–)
Popular as Aragorn in *The Lord of the Rings* films.

9 Helena Christensen (1968–)
Miss Denmark (1986) and a Super Model of the 1990s.

10 Thomas Vinterberg (1969–)
Screenwriter, director and co-founder of Dogme95.

Left **Christians Kirke** Right **Marmorkirken** Right **Sankt Petri Kirke**

🔝10 Churches

1 Helligåndskirken
Dating back to the 12th century, these are among the oldest architectural remains in Copenhagen. Only Helligånds-huset (now used for markets and exhibitions), Christian IV's Baroque portal and Griffenfeld's Chapel survive. Much of the original church burnt down in the fire of 1728. The church re-opened after reconstruction in 1732 (see p16).

2 Christians Kirke
This church was built in the Rococo style in 1755–59 by Nico-lai Eigtved, Frederik V's master architect. It is starkly different from most Danish churches: in-stead of the congregation sitting only in pews in the nave, the church has a second gallery level (like that of a theatre) where all the important worshippers are seated (see p89).

3 Vor Frelsers Kirke
This splendid Baroque church was built in 1682–96 at the behest of Christian V. The king's royal insignia can be seen at various places in the church, including on the organ case that is supported by elephants, the symbol of Denmark's prestigious Order of the Elephant. The spire is 90 m (295 ft) high, and the tower affords a magnificent view of the city. The interior of the church is bright and well-lit, thanks to the white walls and tall windows (see p89).

4 Trinitatis Kirke
Standing next door to the Rundetårn is the Trinitatis Kirke. Commissioned by Christian IV in 1637, this lovely church was completed in the reign of Frederik III in 1656. The present interior dates back to 1731, as the original was burnt in the fire of 1728. It includes boxed pews with seashell carvings, a gilded altarpiece, a Baroque dark wood pulpit and a fabulous gold and silver coloured organ (see p16).

5 Vor Frue Kirke
Also known as St Mary's Cathedral, the church has been on this site in different forms since the 12th century and has played host to royal and national events over the years. The church has a 19th-century façade and a bright interior dominated by statues of Christ and his Apostles (see p16).

Holmens Kirke

6 Sankt Petri Kirke
This is the city's oldest church. Unlike most medieval buildings, it survived the fire of 1728. Its tower, nave and choir date back to the 15th century. The north and south transepts were added in 1634 *(see p16)*.

7 Holmens Kirke
Originally built in 1562 as a naval forge, it was converted into a church in 1619. The Baroque altarpiece is fantastically ornate, and the pulpit is the tallest in Denmark *(see p37)*.

8 Marmorkirken
This circular church has an imposing presence. The dome's interior is covered with paintings of the 12 Apostles and light floods in from 12 skylights. Originally designed by Nicolai Eigtved in 1740, work on the building was suspended in 1770 due to increasing expenses and began again after nearly 150 years, financed by Carl Frederik Tietgen and redesigned by Ferdinand Meldahl. It was finally inaugurated on 19 August 1894 *(see p20)*.

Grundtvigs Kirke

9 Grundtvigs Kirke
This suburban parish church was built in the 1920s–30s by PV Jensen Klint and his son. It has yellow-brick walls and an impressive modern Gothic appearance. To visit take the train to Emdrup. ⓢ På Bjerget 14B, Bispebjerg • 35 81 54 42 • Open 9am–4pm Mon–Wed, Fri & Sat; 9am–6pm Thu; May–Sep noon–4pm Sun; Oct–Apr noon–1pm Sun.

10 Christiansborg Slotskirke
The original 18th-century Rococo creation was destroyed in the palace fire of 1794 and was rebuilt in a Neo-Classical style with a central dome. Inaugurated on Whit Sunday in 1826 to mark the 1,000th anniversary of Christianity in Denmark, it succumbed to another fire in 1992, but has now been rebuilt *(see p28)*.

Further afield, don't miss Roskilde's Gothic brick cathedral which doubles as a mausoleum for the Danish Royal Family, **see p100**.

Left **Det Kongelige Teater** Right **Copenhagen Jazz House**

Performing Art and Music Venues

Operaen

1 Operaen
Famed for its acoustics, the Opera House attracts a variety of international productions. You can enjoy a good view of the stage from any seat and all the seats are relatively cheap due to government subsidy *(see p8)*.

2 Det Kongelige Teater
This is a great destination for a night of entertainment. World-class performances of ballet and drama are held on the old stage in Kongens Nytor *(see p18)* or at the playhouse on the waterfront, Skuespilhuset.

3 Copenhagen Jazz House
Here you can enjoy all kinds of modern jazz – from classic and vocal to electronic, Neo-Bebop and Latin rhythms. There is a bar and a large dance floor as well. Keep an eye out for celebrities. ⊗ *Map J4 • Niels Hemmingsensgade 10 • 33 15 26 00 • www.jazzhouse.dk*

4 Mojo Bluesbar
Smoky, small, dark and intimate, this bar is known for its laidback blues and live jazz performances. There won't be any distracting gimmicks or performance technology on display here. It is very popular, so book ahead. ⊗ *Map H5 • Løngangstræde 21C • 33 11 64 53; Booking: 23 44 97 77 • www.mojo.dk*

5 Wallmans Saloner
This circular former circus building (1884) is now a glamorous venue offering old-fashioned "dinner, show and dancing". There is surround-entertainment on seven stages while resting members of the cast serve you a good dinner. After the show, it turns into a nightclub. ⊗ *Map G5 • Cirkusbyninger Jernbanegade 8 • 33 16 37 00 • www.wallmans.dk*

6 Tivoli Concert Hall
The Tivoli Concert Hall is the city's largest music venue, with capacity of 1,900. It stages over 100 operas, ballets, rock and jazz concerts during the Tivoli season *(see p11)*.

Mojo Bluesbar

Tivoli Concert Hall

7 Det Ny Teater
This early 20th-century theatre hosts popular international musicals, such as *Phantom of the Opera* and *Les Misérables*. ◎ *Map C5 • Gammel Kongevej 29 • 33 25 50 75 • www.detnyteater.dk*

8 Koncerthuset
The concert house of national broadcaster Danmarks Radio (DR), was designed by Jean Nouvel. Located in DR-Byen (broadcasting city) in the Ørestad district, this landmark building with its blue glass façade has superior acoustics. ◎ *Map B3 • Emil Holms Kanal 20 • 35 20 30 40 • www.dr.dk/koncerthuset*

9 Parken
This football stadium held its first indoor concert in 2001 with the Eurovision Song Concert. Famous bands like U2, Metallica and Madonna have performed here since. ◎ *Map D2*

10 Loppen
This is the best indie rock venue in town. Bands like Franz Ferdinand, Interpol and Antony & the Johnsons performed here long before they hit the big time. ◎ *Map M5 • Bådsmandsstræde 43, Christianshavn • 32 57 84 22 • Open 9pm–late • www.loppen.dk*

Top 10 Jazz Venues and Events

1 Bars and Cafés
Popular places include Christianhavn's Sofie Kælderen *(see p93)* and Nørrebro's Café Blågårds Apotek.

2 Pumpehuset
Music venue around the side of Axeltorv seating 600. ◎ *Studiestræde 52 • 33 93 19 60*

3 Jazzhus Montmartre
This legendary venue seats just 70 people. ◎ *Store Renegade 19a • 31 72 34 94*

4 La Fontaine
Known for late sessions, from 11pm Fri–Sat. ◎ *Kompagnistræde 11 • 33 11 60 98*

5 Huset Magstræde
This city-council funded culture house hosts a regular jazz club on the first floor. ◎ *Rådhusstræde 13 • 33 69 32 00*

6 Jazzcup
Both a record store and a café, Jazzcup hosts regular jazz sessions and is good for experimental jazz. ◎ *Gothersgade 107 • 33 15 02 02*

7 M/S Stubnitz
A 1964 steel ferry hosting concerts and parties during the jazz festival. ◎ *Havnegade, Kaj Plads 141 • 28 78 41 98*

8 Tango y Vinos
This wine bar has a dance floor and hosts a number of jazz nights. ◎ *Herluf Trolles Gade 9 • 33 32 81 16*

9 Copenhagen Jazz Festival
For 10 days in July, jazz spills out onto the streets, squares and historic buildings.

10 Winter Jazz
An extension of the jazz festival, this smaller programme takes place in Jan–Feb.

Left **A brunch café in Halmtorvet** Right **Cyclists relaxing by Rosenborg Slot**

Outdoor Activities

A harbour trip

Bikes
Almost every major road in Copenhagen has a cycle lane and you can hire a bike *(see p106)* for a day or more. In summer, you can hop onto a free City Bike (provided for a refundable fee by the city of Copenhagen across 125 City Bike Parking places) and ride within city limits.

Harbour Trips
Harbour trips are a lovely way to see the city. There are two canal tour companies *(see p8)*; both begin trips at Nyhavn. You can also tour the city on a harbour bus. If you are carrying a Copenhagen Card *(see p111)*, you can change buses using just a single ticket.

Outdoor Dining
In the 1990s, Copenhagen witnessed a surge in outdoor dining venues. Now, virtually all cafés and restaurants offer outdoor dining in the summer. Blankets and heaters are provided for when it gets chilly. Nyhavn and Peblinge Dossering offer particularly good views.

Flea Markets
There are many outdoor flea markets in the summer, offering everything from furniture and clothing to pseudo-antiques and retro vinyl.
⊗ *Frederiksberg Rådhusplads: Map A5; 8am–3pm Sat • Gamme Strand: Map J4; 8am–5pm Fri–Sa • Kongens Nytorv: Map K4; 9am–5pm Sat • Nørrebrogade: Map C3; 10am–4pm Sat*

Tivoli
At Tivoli, you can wander through the stalls, check out the rides, listen to the Tivoli bands (free rock and pop concerts on Friday nights), or simply relax on a lakeside bench *(see pp10–11)*.

Lounging by the Lakes
Man-made lakes divide the main city from Nørrebro and Østerbro. Of these, Skt Jørgens

Flea market at Gammel Strand

oologisk Have

ø, Peblinge Sø and Sortedam
Sø are easily accessible. You can
ounge along their grassy banks
r enjoy the scenic view from
he bridges that cross them.

Dyrehaven
This deer park (it does still
ave lots of deer – the rutting
eason is in the autumn), has
een here since the 16th
entury. It is like an English
ark or common and features
 noisy, enjoyable fun fair, called
akken. For a bit of excitement,
ake a pony and trap ride. ❧ *Map*
2 • Dyrehaven Klampenborg • www.
akken.dk

Kongens Have
Attached to Rosenborg Slot,
he King's Garden is a great
lace to sunbathe, play frisbee,
ricket, football or have a picnic.
 the summer, you can catch a
uppet show or a jazz concert
see pp14–15).

Assistens Kirkegård
This beautiful, meandering
hurchyard holds the graves of
amous Danes like HC Andersen,
ugust Bournonville and Niels
ohr *(see p75).*

Zoologisk Have
You will find polar bears,
ons, tigers, elephants and other
nimals in this delightful zoo.
here are thematic adventure
ails for kids *(see p83).*

Top 10 Beaches and Pools

1 Havnebadet
Popular floating harbour
pool with fresh water. ❧ *Islands
Brygge • 23 71 31 89*

2 Bellevue
Full of people playing,
sailing or relaxing. Left end is
nudist. ❧ *Strandvejen 340, 2930
Klampenborg*

3 Fælledparkens Soppesø
Huge, child-friendly outdoor
pool. ❧ *Borgmester Jensens
Allé 50, Østerbro • 33 66 36 60*

4 Amager Strandpark
Luxury Beach with lagoon,
artificial island and snack
kiosks. ❧ *Amager Strandvej
• www.amager-strand.dk*

5 Køge Bugt Strandpark
A 7 km (4 mile) beach along
Køge Bay from Brøndby to
Hundige. ❧ *Ishøj Store Torv 20,
2635 Ishøj*

6 Bellahøj Svømmestadion
Indoor and outdoor swimming
facilities, including waterslides.
❧ *Bellahøjvej 1–3, Brønshøj
• 38 26 21 40*

7 Frederiksdal Friluftsbad
Gorgeous lakeside beach
with café. ❧ *Frederiksdal
Badesti 1, Virum • 45 83 81 85*

8 DGI-Byen
Indoor facilities with a
"super-ellipse" pool and a kids'
pool. ❧ *Corner of Tietgensgade
& Ingerslevsgade • 33 29 81 40*

9 Charlottenlund Beach
Good place for sunbathing.
❧ *Park Strandvejen 144,
Charlottenlund*

10 Copencabana Havnebadet ved Fisketorvet
Includes a floating harbour
pool and three outdoor pools.
❧ *Havneholmen 0, Vesterbro
• 27 52 90 28*

Copenhagen's Top 10

For more outdoor activities beyond Copenhagen, see pp96–102.

Left **Girlie Hurley Shop** Centre **Shopping street, Strøget (north)** Right **Shop front, Bredgade**

🔟 Shopping Districts

1 Strøget
Copenhagen's shopping street is known by many simply as 'the walking street'. The shops, which stretch across five linked pedestrian streets, range from cheerful and inexpensive outlets to designer and upmarket department stores (towards Kongens Nytorv). It has something for everyone, from bargain clothes to exclusive silver, porcelain and glassware of the Royal Scandinavia shops. Strøget is also popular for its street performers *(see p66)*.

2 Off Strøget (North)
Heading up north from Strøget, you will find numerous little boutiques, record stores and second-hand shops. Indulge in some individual shopping on streets like Skindergade, Larsbjørnstræde, Vestergade, Studiestræde and Sankt Peders Stræde. ◈ *Map H4–J4*

Strøget

Glam clothes shop in Nørrebro

3 Off Strøget (South)
The streets to the south of Strøget are great for "alternative" shopping. Læderstræde and Kompagnistræde are especially good, the latter most for its antique shops. ◈ *Map J4–J*

4 Kronprinsensgade
This posh shopping area includes many of Scandinavia's top designer brands, such as St P and Bruuns Bazaar. You will also find Scandinavia's oldest tea shop, Perch's Tea Room. ◈ *Map J*

5 Nansensgade
Located on the outskirts of the old town, this area has a mix of traditional and trendy boutiques, as well as good restaurants and cafés. ◈ *Map G3*

6 Nørrebro
Although this area is not as trendy as it once was, it still has many second-hand stores and chic boutiques. Check out the shops to the east of the Assistens Cemetery around Sankt Hans Torv. ◈ *Map D3*

For more shopping alternatives, **see pp80, 86, 92.**

7 Vesterbro

This former red light area is now a gritty shopping district offering good bargains. Among the more interesting streets are Istedgade, which is lined with boutiques and art shops and Værnedamsvej, which has several independent fashion stores and gourmet food shops. ✆ *Map C5–C6*

8 Frederiksberg

Along Gammel Kongevej, Frederiksberg's main thoroughfare, you will find excellent shops catering to affluent tastes with prices to match. ✆ *Map B5*

9 Fisketorv Shopping Centre

Situated on the waterfront facing the Inner Harbour, this city mall is a few minutes away from the Copencabana harbour pool *(see p45)*. It has over 120 shops, several restaurants and a multiplex cinema. ✆ *Map J6* • *Kalvebod Brygge 59, Vesterbro • 35 37 19 17 • Open 10am–8pm Mon–Fri, 10am–5pm Sat, first Sunday of the month*

10 Bredgade

If you are looking for traditional, pre-20th-century antiques, this is the perfect place to visit. Here you will find several grand-looking shops and auction houses that sell all kinds of antiques, including authentic paintings and statues. ✆ *Map L3*

Kronprinsensgade

Top 10 Danish Design Companies

1 Kjærholm furniture
Poul Kjærholm designed functional coffee tables and chairs, all named simply PK with a number. Production continues under the leadership of his son, Thomas.

2 Cylinda-Line (by Arne Jacobsen)
Popular tableware collection (1967). Combines steel, wood and plastic.

3 Bang & Olufsen
Known for their cutting-edge audio-visual designs. ✆ *www.bang-olufsen.com*

4 Kaare Klint Furniture
Combines ergonomics with elegant 18th-century English styles.

5 Bodum
Classic and smart kitchen-ware in steel and glass. ✆ *www.bodum.com*

6 Lego
These popular building blocks were introduced in 1952. ✆ *www.lego.com*

7 Vipp
Designers of a classic stainless steel pedal bin, Vipp's products also include soap dishes and dispensers. ✆ *www.vipp.dk*

8 Flora Danica Porcelain
Royal porcelain design featuring floral motifs. ✆ *www.royalcopenhagen.com*

9 Poul Henningsen Lamps
Famous lamp design, creating the effect of maximum light and minimum shadow.

10 Georg Jensen Silverware
Original, organic tableware designs and casual jewellery. ✆ *www.georgjensen.com*

Left **Formel B** Right **Le Sommelier**

🔟 Restaurants

1 Restaurant Herman
Seating just 40 guests, this exclusive restaurant is named after head chef Thomas Herman, who transforms traditional Danish dishes like *brændende kærlighed* (mashed potatoes, bacon and onions) into a gourmet adventure. ⊗ *Map G6 • Bernstoffsgade 5 • 88 70 00 20 • Open noon–1:30pm & 6pm–midnight Mon–Fri, 6pm–midnight Sat • Closed for Lunch Jan–Mar • www.nimb.dk • ⊛⊛⊛⊛⊛*

2 Umami
While the slick, contemporary design and attentive service here are noteworthy, it is the food that stands out. The delicate flavours that arise from combining Japanese and French cuisines have to be experienced to be believed. ⊗ *Map K3 • Store Kongensgade 59 • 33 38 75 00 • Open 6–10pm Sun–Thu, 6–11pm Fri–Sat • www.restaurantumami.dk • ⊛⊛⊛⊛⊛*

Frikadeller

3 Kong Hans Kælder
This unique restaurant has white-washed, underlit arches in Copenhagen's oldest building. Watch the chef in the open kitchen as he cooks up fancy dishes from the à la carte and fixed-price menus. ⊗ *Map K4 • Vingårdsstræde 6 • 33 32 62 63 • Open 6pm–midnight Mon–Sat • www.konghans.dk • ⊛⊛⊛⊛⊛*

4 AOC
Dine with class in the romantic and elegant surroundings of the 18th-century Moltkes Palace basement. AOC's name stands for Arrø & Co, after sommelier and owner Christian Aarø. The inventive set courses are perfectly presented and have earned the restaurant a Michelin star. ⊗ *Map K3 • Dronningens Tværgade 2 • 33 11 11 45 • www.aaro-co.dk • ⊛⊛⊛⊛⊛*

5 Era Ora
Umbrian cuisine is served in this well-established Italian restaurant. Enjoy lunchtime al fresco dining or fuller evening menus (of 12–17 small dishes) in this 18th-century building's warmly decorated room. Several combined food and wine lists are also available for up to 3,800kr *(see p93)*.

6 Godt
The modest blue-painted exterior conceals a fabulous dining experience at this appropriately named ("good") restaurant. The English chef regularly wanders amongst the 20-seater restaurant adding that personal touch to this husband-wife enterprise. ⊗ *Map K3 • Gothersgade 38 • 33 15 21 22 • Open 6pm–midnight Tue–Sat • ⊛⊛⊛⊛⊛*

For more restaurants and a key to price categories, see pp67, 71, 79, 87, 93, 103.

Noma

Voted world's best restaurant
y *Restaurant* magazine, Noma
ffers superior Nordic fare
ourced from Denmark, Iceland,
reenland and the Faroe Islands.
un by chef René Redzepi, the
estaurant is housed in a
abulous warehouse dating from
767. The interior has a northern
habby chic look with open
eams. It is Denmark's only
-star restaurant to have been
eatured in the Michelin Guide
see p93).

Le Sommelier

A first-rate French restaurant,
with impeccable staff, a pleasant
tmosphere and a massive wine
st. The *foie gras* is delicious. In
he right season, be sure to try
he seafood. The chocolate plate
den with five different
hocolate-inspired confections is
ard to resist. ⊗ *Map L3 • Bredgade*
3–65 • 33 11 45 15 • Open noon–2pm &
-10pm Mon–Thu, noon–2pm & 6–11pm
i, 6–11pm Sat, 6–10pm Sun
www.lesommelier.dk • ®®®®

Formel B

Beautifully prepared, French-
tyle cuisine using fresh Danish
gredients is the key to the
asty dishes served in this
harming restaurant. Winter fare
cludes raw marinated shrimps
ith squid and soy-ginger
rowned butter *(see p87)*.

Meet the Danes

If you fancy some good,
aditional Danish home cooking
nd want to see how the locals
ve, Meet the Danes is an
rganization that gives you
e opportunity to do just
at. A must-stop for groups
nd independent travellers.
 Map G4–H5 • Vester Voldgade 85
23 28 43 47 • www.meetthedanes.dk

Top 10 Danish dishes

1 Frikadeller
Pork and veal meatballs,
fried in butter and usually
served with potatoes.

2 Stegt Flæsk
A classic Danish dish.
Fried slices of pork on the
bone with a creamy parsley
sauce and potatoes.

3 Smørrebrødsmad
An open sandwich usually
made with rye bread. Beef
with horseradish sauce is a
popular topping.

4 Skipperlabskovs
Beef, marinated for 24
hours in brine and stewed
with potatoes, bay leaves
and black peppercorns.

5 Sol Over Gudhjem
A typical Bornholm dish.
Smoked herring, topped with
egg yolk, onion and chives.

6 Marinerede Sild
Herring, marinated in
vinegar and spices, served
with onion and capers. Tastes
best with rye bread.

7 Rødkål
A common way of cooking
Rødkål (red cabbage) is stew-
ing it for 40 minutes with
apples, vinegar and sugar.

8 Kogt Hamburgerryg
A Danish staple of pork
loin cooked with thyme and
parsley, accompanied by
boiled potatoes, vegetables;
horseradish or mustard sauce
is often added for taste.

9 Ris à l'Amande
Rice pudding with
almonds, served cold and
topped with warm cherry
sauce. A popular Christmas-
time dessert.

10 Gulerodskage
Carrot cake made with
walnuts and often served
with whipped cream.

Left **Thé à la Menthe** Right **Emmerys Bakery**

🔟 Cafés and Bars

Laundromat Café

Bastionen and Løven
Set inside an old mill in Christianshavn, this is one of the most romantic eateries in Copenhagen. It is famous for its weekend brunches, so try to get there early *(see p93)*.

Laundromat Café
There is a lot you can do at this cheerful, "hybrid" café. You can pop your laundry into one of the Laundromat machines and relax with a cup of coffee, or have lunch. You can also browse through the newspapers and the hundreds of books on display. ⊗ *Map C3 • Elmegade 15, Nørrebro • 35 35 26 72 • www.thelaundromatcafe.com • ⓚ*

Emmerys Bakery
This is Denmark's foremost organic gourmet store. Primarily a bakery, it is also known to sell sandwiches, drinks and an array of beautifully packaged gourmet food. It has a nice café area where you can sample their goods, anytime from breakfast onwards *(see p86)*.

Rabes Have
This 17th-century pub has a tasteful decor, with dark green and white wall and a pretty garden at the back. The food served her is mostly organic and tradtional open sandwiches ar offered at lunchtime. In th summer, it also provides catering services to Kunst industrimuseet *(see p93)*.

Pussy Galore's Flying Circus
This is one of the first cafés to have opened in trendy Nørrebro They serve good food and in the summer, you can sit out on the cobbled square and enjoy your snack *(see p79)*.

Kontiki Bar & Færgen Elle
This refreshing bar is set on a boat, just behind the Opera House on Holmen. Located far from the bustle of busy tourist areas, you can sit out on the deck for drinks and snacks, or have a more formal meal in the cabin. It is advisable to book ahead. ⊗ *Map M4 • Takkelloftvej 1Z • Open May–Sep only • 40 50 90 48 • www.kontikibar.dk • ⓚⓚ*

Cafe Retro
This non-profit café just off Strøget, is run by an international group of volunteers. It offers soup, tapas, cake and ho and cold drinks at low prices. Spread over two floors, the decor consists of comfortable

Pussy Galore's Flying Circus

...ofas and candle-lit coffee tables.
• Map J4 • Knabrostræde 26 • Open
noon–11pm Tue–Thu and Sun, noon–1am
Fri–Sat • Closed Mon • www.cafe-retro.
dk • ®

Thé à la Menthe
This lovely little basement
Moroccan tea salon offers great
old drinks, tea and meze, as
well as serving warm Moroccan
dishes, salads and samosas. The
decor is Moroccan, with kilms
and water-pipes. Yet, it retains a
Danish feel with cream-coloured
wall panelling and pale green
divans. • Map J5 • Rådhusstræde 5b
• 33 33 00 38 • ®

Salonen
This wonderfully cosy café is
a firm favourite with both
international students and locals.
The laid-back atmosphere makes
Salonen a great place to lounge
and relax with a large cup of
coffee or tea. For those in need
of greater sustenance, the
friendly staff serve up hearty
food from the fusion/crossover
menu – prepared in a kitchen
little bigger than a square metre.
There are DJs at the weekend.
• Map H4 • Sankt Peders Stræde 20
• 50 19 18 11 • Open 11am–1am Mon–Sat,
11am–midnight Sun • ®

La Glace
Located just off Strøget, La
Glace is one of the foremost
(and the oldest) confectioneries
in Copenhagen, offering mouth-
watering cakes and chocolates.
Both coffee and cakes are
beautifully presented, and they
are best savoured in the Old-
World ambience created by the
traditional polished-wood interiors.
• Map H4 • Skoubogade 3–5 • 33 14 46
46 • Open 8:30am–5:30pm Mon–Thu,
8:30am–6pm Fri, 9am–5pm Sat
(also 11am–5pm Sun Sep–Easter)
• www.laglace.dk • ®

The interior of La Glace

For more cafés and bars, see pp52–5, 79, 81 and 93.

A night out at Culture Box

Nightlife Venues

Søpavillonen

1 Søpavillonen
Great tribute bands perform at this stunning lakeside pavilion, that has been transformed into a restaurant, bar and spacious dance floor. DJs play a mix of '70s and '80s disco, with elements of Latin, rock and Danish pop.
◈ Map C4 • Gyldenløvesgade 24 • 33 15 12 24 • Nightclub: 11pm–5am Fri–Sat • Over 18s only • www.soepavillonen.dk

2 Rust
Trendy Rust is at the cutting edge of the local music and clubbing scene. It showcases up-and-coming acts and top international DJs playing an eclectic mix of sounds. ◈ Map C3 • Guldbergsgade 8 • 35 24 52 00 • Open 9pm–5am Wed–Sat • Nightclub min age: Wed–Thu 18, Fri–Sat 20 • www.rust.dk

3 Park Diskotek
This sophisticated venue plays an exciting range of music. There are several dance floors here. ◈ Map E2 • Østerbrogade 79 • 70 33 32 22 • Open 11pm–5am Fri, 11pm–6am Sat • Min age: Fri 20, Sat 23 • Dress code • www.park.dk

4 The Rock
This club offers the total rock experience – from heavy metal and hard rock to rock'n'roll Set inside a sprawling former courthouse, it has four bars, a huge stage and a welcoming atmosphere. For those with a preference for reggae and hip-hop tunes, events and even live concerts are held during the week (see p70).

5 Barbarellah
This Latin restaurant and cocktail bar in the bohemian Nørrensgade district is great for late night drinks and music. There's no entry charge. ◈ Map G3 • Nørre Farimagsgade 41 • 33 32 00 61 • Oper 2pm–2am Tue–Thu, 2pm–4am Fri–Sat • Closed Sun–Mon • www.barbarellah.o

6 Gefährlich
Located in the heart of Norrebro, known for its club culture, Gefährlich (German for "dangerous") has a restaurant, bar, art gallery, coffee shop, boutique and record store. Its nightclub caters to the tastes of the young and hip (see p81).

Rust

For more nightlife venues, see pp70, 81.

Club Mambo

VEGA
7 Housed in a 1950s trade union building the club, Nina Bang, exudes a Scandinavian atmosphere and attracts international acts and DJs. The Ideal Bar is on the ground floor.
🅂 Map B6 • Enghavevej 40 • 33 25 70 11 • Nina Bang: Open 11pm–4am Fri–Sat; min age 21; adm: 60kr after 1am • Ideal Bar: Open 10pm–4am Wed, 10pm–5am Thu–Sat • www.vega.dk

Culture Box
8 This purist techno club is one of Copenhagen's leading venues for electronic music. 🅂 Map K2 • Kronprinsessegade 54 • 33 32 50 50 • Open 9pm–4am Wed, 10pm–4am Thu, midnight–6am Fri–Sat • Closed Jun–Jul • Min age 18 • www.culture-box.com

Nord Natklub
9 A popular nightclub catering exclusively for the over-30s and located in the brightly coloured Palads building. Free entry for Tivoli ticket holders on Fridays, for post-concert parties. 🅂 Map G5 • Axeltorv 5 • Open 10pm–5am Fri–Sat • Adm • www.nordnatklub.dk

Club Mambo
10 This is the place to "feel the Latin spirit". An energetic and colourful club, it is one of the hottest salsa clubs in the city. Take advantage of the hour long, free salsa and merengue classes on offer at the club (see p70).

Top 10 Microbreweries

1 Mikkeller
This microbrewery was started in 2006 and has its own pub. 🅂 Viktoriagade 8, Vesterbro • 31 66 24 44 • www.mikkeller.dk

2 Nørrebro Bryghus
Take a tour of the brewery; taste some beer. 🅂 Ryesgade 3, Nørrebro • 35 30 05 30 • www.noerrebrobryghus.dk

3 Vesterbro Bryghus
Six beers brewed to traditional Austrian recipes. 🅂 Vesterbrogade 2B • 33 11 17 05 • www.vesterbrobryghus.dk

4 Færgekroen
Two hand-brewed beers on offer. 🅂 Tivoli • 33 75 06 80 • www.faergekroen.dk

5 Brewpub
Beer garden in a 17th-century building. 🅂 Vestergade 29 • 33 32 00 60 • Closed Sun • www.brewpub.dk

6 Bryggeriet Apollo
One of the original local microbreweries. 🅂 Vesterbrogade 3 • 33 12 33 13

7 Herslev Bryghus
This small brewery has a shop in its yard (open 1–6pm Fri). 🅂 Kattingevej 8, Herslev, Roskilde • 46 40 18 07

8 Fuglebjerggaard
Organic microbrewery on a farm, run by TV cook Camilla Plum. 🅂 Hemmingstrupvej 8, Helsingør • 46 39 39 43

9 Amager Bryghus
Tours on Mon–Sat by appointment only. 🅂 Fuglebækvej 2C • 32 50 62 00

10 Copenhagen Beer Festival
Beer festival held each May in an old Carlsberg tapping plant. 🅂 Tap 1, Ny Carlsbergvej 91, Vesterbro • www.beerfestival.dk

Left **Centralhjørnet** Right **Masken Bar & Café**

Gay and Lesbian Venues

1 Centralhjørnet
This is Copenhagen's oldest gay bar, dating from 1852. It holds drag nights; regular shows take place on Thursdays. Kylie Minogue and Europop are jukebox favourites. Sunday afternoons are usually packed. 🅂 *Map H4 • Kattesundet 18 • 33 11 85 49 • Open noon–2am • www.centralhjornet.dk*

2 Dunkel
The atmospheric lighting (Dunkel means "slightly dark" in Danish) and stuffed owls on the ceiling are set off by the electronic music that bounces off the black walls. The broad beer selection caters to the hip young crowd. 🅂 *Map H5 • Vester Voldgade 10 • 33 14 13 30 • Open 11pm–5am Thu–Sat*

3 Jailhouse
Kitted out as a prison, this café and event bar has booths like prison cells and staff dressed as prison guards or police officers. There is a restaurant on the second floor; the atmosphere here is more sedate. 🅂 *Map H4 • Studiestræde 12 • 33 15 22 55 • Open 3pm–2am Sun–Thu, 3pm–5am Fri–Sat; Restaurant: 6–11pm Thu–Sat • www.jailhousecph.dk*

4 Oscar Bar and Café
A bar and café for the style-conscious, it has a 2-m (almost 7-ft) long bar and posh leather furniture. The DJ plays funky disco and soulful deep house on weekends. 🅂 *Map H5 • Rådhus pladsen 77 • 33 12 09 99 • Open noon–midnight Sun–Wed, noon–2am Thu–Fri (kitchen till 10pm) • www.oscarbarcafe.dk*

5 Café Intime's Piano Bar
Founded in 1913, this kitsch bar has a predominantly gay crowd. A pianist plays popular classics (don't be afraid to sing along); you can also enjoy jazz on Sundays. 🅂 *Map B5 • Allégade 25, 2000 Frederiksberg • 38 34 19 58 • Open 6pm–2am daily • www.cafeintime.dk*

6 Amigo Bar
This popular bar pulsates with a lively party atmosphere well into the early hours. Its speciality is camp karaoke. 🅂 *Map C5 • Schønbergsgade 4, 2000 Frederiksberg • 33 21 49 15 • Open 10pm–7am daily*

7 K3
This three-storey "pansexual" club caters to a range of crowds during the week, with four rooms,

Jailhouse

Oscar Bar and Café

wo dance floors and electronic pop from the 1970s, '80s and 90s blasting out of the sound system. There is a minimum age limit of 24 on Saturdays. ⊗ Map J4 • Knabostræde 3 • 33 14 13 30 • Open 10pm–6am Thu–Sat • www.k-3.dk

8 Mens Bar
This strictly all-male, no-frills bar is filled with leather, fascinating tattoos and a dash of denim. Try to catch the free Danish brunch at 3pm on the first Sunday of the month. ⊗ Map H4 • Teglgardsstræde 3 • 33 12 73 03 • Open 3pm–2am daily • www. mensbar.dk

9 Masken Bar & Café
The younger crowd at this venue starts buzzing after midnight. It has exciting live music and drag shows, spread across two floors. ⊗ Map H4 • Studiestræde 33 • 33 91 09 37 • Open 4pm–2am Mon–Thu, 4pm–5am Fri, 3pm–5am Sat, 3pm–2am Sun • www.maskenbar.dk

10 Meet Gay Copenhagen
You can meet and dine with local gays and lesbians in the comfort of their homes. Hosts are very friendly and usually offer traditional fare. It's best to book a dinner well in advance. Note: this is not a dating agency. ⊗ 27 21 80 65 • www.meetgaycopenhagen.dk

Top 10 Gay & Lesbian Festivals & Events

1 Copenhagen Gay & Lesbian Film Festival
10-day film festival, usually in October, at various venues. ⊗ 33 93 07 66 • www.cglff.dk

2 Copenhagen Pride Festival
Week-long festival in August. Includes the gay pride parade. ⊗ www.copenhagenpride.dk

3 Mr Gay
Pan Club's popular, good-humoured beauty pageant for gays. ⊗ www.mrgay.dk

4 Rainbow Festival
10 days of art exhibitions, drag shows, dancing and parades just across the bridge at Malmö, Sweden. ⊗ www.rfsl.se/malmo

5 World Aids Day
Commemorated each year on 1 Dec.

6 Copenhagen Mermates
Gay and lesbian swimming club with swim and water polo evenings at four different pools in Copenhagen. ⊗ www.mermates.dk

7 Nordic Open
Dance competition for same-sex couples on 30 December every year. ⊗ www.pandans.dk/nordicopen.htm

8 Torchlight Procession
This event in memory of people who have died of AIDS takes place on the last Sunday in May. ⊗ www.aidsfondet.dk

9 St. Hans
Annual bonfire and beach party on Amager Beach on Sankt Hans Night, 23 June. ⊗ www.lbl.dk

10 Queer Festival
Musicians, activists and drag kings and queens take part. ⊗ www.queerfestival.org

Left **Children's Museum at the Nationalmuseet** Right **Classic car rides, Tivoli**

🔟 Places for Children

Guinness World Records Museum

1 Guinness World Records Museum
This highly popular attraction brings the Guinness World Records to life. From the bizarre, such as bicycle-eating men to the internationally renowned in sport and science, 13 galleries celebrate strangeness, ingenuity and determination (see p66).

2 Statens Museum for Kunst
The Children's Art Museum of the Danish National Gallery holds exhibitions for children between the ages of 6 and 12. Artist-led workshops are designed to allow children to develop ideas in response to art at the museum (see pp22–3).

3 Wonderful World of HC Andersen Museum
Explore the life of Hans Christian Andersen, Denmark's national hero, at this charming museum. It is aimed at kids who will enjoy the tableaux and recordings of some of his fairytales (in several languages). The hand-written manuscript of *The Stone and the Wise Man* (1858) may interest bibliophiles (see p66).

4 Nationalmuseet
The National Museum includes an interesting Children's Museum. Rather than just looking at things, children are encouraged to participate in numerous activities, like dressing up in grandma's clothes to see how different they are from today's garments, or sitting in an old Danish classroom, learning about medieval castles (see pp26–7).

5 Tøjhusmuseet
The Royal Arsenal Museum, on the island of Slotsholmen, is a popular tourist site and is home to Christian IV's original arsenal (1604–8). The ground floor, in particular, evokes the atmosphere of those days, with a long arched cavern and canons along walls (see p28).

Hands-on fun for kids at Experimentarium

6 Experimentarium

This innovative science centre brings science to life through hands-on exploration. Most exhibits are interactive, allowing kids to perform 300 different experiments. Environmental issues are high on the agenda and adults will have as much fun as the kids. ✆ *Map B2*
• *Tuborg Havnevej 7, Hellerup* • *39 27 33 33*
• *Open 9:30am–7pm Mon–Fri (to 9pm Tue), 11am–5pm Sat–Sun & hols* • *Adm charges; free for 0–2 year olds* • *Dis access* • *www.experimentarium.dk*

7 Danmarks Akvarium

Over 70 tanks of the world's most exotic fish are found here. Touchtanks let you get closer to the safer marine life. Turtles, piranhas and sharks are the star attractions *(see p99)*.

Dried seahorse, Danmarks Akvarium

8 Zoologisk Have

This zoo is Denmark's largest cultural institution, attracting around 1.2 million visitors every year. Besides the tigers, polar bears and elephants, there are thematic adventure trails and a children's petting zoo. In spring, there tend to be many new baby animals *(see p83)*.

9 Tivoli

The best time to take kids to Tivoli is during the day, when the atmosphere is more family-oriented. The many fun rides include cars on tracks, dragon boats on the lake, the pantomime theatre and the trolley bus. There are changing facilities, and plenty of child-friendly places to eat *(see pp10–13)*.

10 Ripley's Believe It or Not!

While adults may find the collection of bizarre, freakish curiosities on display a little unsettling, kids are sure to love it! The Ecuadorian shrunken heads are a particularly gruesome highlight. ✆ *Map H5*
• *Rådhuspladsen 57* • *33 32 31 31*
• *Open 10am–6pm daily (to 8pm Fri–Sat)*
• *Adm; Copenhagen Card accepted*

Left **Christian VIII's Palace, Amalienborg** Right **Vor Frue Kirke, detail of façade**

Sights of Royal Copenhagen

1 Amalienborg

This royal residence consists of four palaces arranged around a square. Two of the Palaces function as museums and are open to the public, while the other two are royal homes and remain closed. Queen Margrethe resides in Christian IX's Palace and Crown Prince Frederik in Frederik VIII's Palace. An interesting museum housed in Christian VIII's Palace includes reconstructed rooms from the 19th century *(see pp20–21)*.

2 Rosenborg Slot

This delightful, turreted Renaissance palace, built by Christian IV, is the oldest royal palace standing in its original form. It is also a depository for the crown jewels *(see pp14–15)*.

3 Royal Copenhagen Porcelain

This was one of the first porcelain factories outside Germany.

Christiansborg Slot

The traditional Royal Copenhagen design, "Blue Floral", dates back to the factory's initiation in 1775. The pottery features a blue design because in earlier times, cobalt was the only colour that was able to withstand high firing temperatures *(see p68)*.

4 Vor Frue Kirke

St. Mary's Cathedral has been a place of royal worship and ceremony since the 12th century, when Margrethe I married Håkon IV of Norway. Since then, Christian I (1449) and Crown Prince Frederik (2004) have been married here and several princes have been crowned *(see p17)*.

5 Christiansborg Slot

This is the seventh castle to have been built upon this site. The first, Bishop Absalon's fortified castle (1167), was destroyed in 1369. It has since been rebuilt several times. The castle built in 1730 was the first to be called Christiansborg; it was destroyed by fire 64 years later *(see p28)*.

6 Crown Jewels

These symbols of monarchy, kept in the stronghold basement of Rosenborg Slot, include the crown, sceptre, orb, sword of state, ampulla (flask for anointing the monarch) and royal jewellery.

7 Fredensborg Slot

This 18th-century Baroque palace is the Queen's summer

Rosenborg Slot

and autumn home. The beautiful gardens are among Denmark's largest. ✆ 33 40 31 87 • *Open only in Jul 1pm–4:30pm; Reserved gardens: 9am–5pm • Adm; free entry to gardens • Bus 173E, direction Fredensborg*

8 Frederiksborg Slot
Christian IV built this Dutch Renaissance-style castle between 1600–20. It is notable for its spires, copper roofs and sweeping gables. After being destroyed in a fire in 1859, the Carlsberg Brewery magnate, Jacob Jacobsen, helped rebuild it. The gardens, dating to 1720–25, were the only royal gardens to have escaped being updated to the 19th-century Romantic style *(see pp98–9).*

9 Roskilde Domkirke
Danish royals, including Harald Bluetooth *(see p33)*, have been buried here since the 12th century. It now houses 39 tombs, the oldest belonging to Margrethe I (d. 1412) *(see p100).*

10 Kronborg Slot
This castle, built as a fortress in the 15th century, was used as a prison and army barracks until 1922. It is now occasionally used for royal functions. You may even hear a salute being fired whenever the royal yacht passes by *(see p102).*

The Treasury

1 Christian IV's Crown
Made in 1595–96 by Dirich Fyring, with diamond, gold, enamel and pearls.

2 The Queen's Crown
Made for Queen Sophie Magdalene in 1731. The large, square table-cut diamonds are believed to have come from Queen Sophie Amalie's crown (1648).

3 Christian V's Crown
Christian V's Absolutist crown (1670–71). Its large, rare sapphire is believed to be a present from the Duke of Milan to Christian I in 1474.

4 The Regalia
Sceptre, orb, globe and ampulla made for Frederik III's coronation. Used at subsequent coronations until 1840.

5 Order of the Elephant
Founded by Christian I around 1450. The chain is made of gold, enamel, diamonds and pearls.

6 Order of the Dannebrog
Established in 1671 as part of the measures introduced by the Absolute monarchs to manage their subjects.

7 Jewellery Sets
Includes pearl set (1840), made from Charlotte Amalie's jewellery; diamond set (18th century); emerald set (1723).

8 The Oldenburg Horn
Enamelled, silver-gilt drinking horn (around 1465).

9 The King's Law 1665
Absolutism's constitution, made from parchment, silk, gold and silver.

10 Baptismal Set
Four-piece, gold and silver baptismal set (1671), thought to have been first used for Crown Prince Frederik.

AROUND TOWN

COPENHAGEN'S TOP 10

Left **Ny Carlsberg Glyptotek** Right **Kongens Nytorv**

Tivoli North to Gothersgade

RICH IN HISTORY, *this area is a popular entertainment destination. Heading north-northeast of Tivoli, which was originally outside the city walls, you can walk back in time through the old town that evolved during the Middle Ages – though much of it succumbed to fire in the 18th century – to Slotsholmen, the site where the first dwellings that became Copenhagen were built in the 12th century. Along the way, you will find great shopping areas, museums, an old town and a royal palace.*

🔟 Sights

1. Tivoli
2. Rådhuset
3. Astronomical Clock
4. Ny Carlsberg Glyptotek
5. Nationalmuseet
6. Dansk Design Centre
7. Amagertov
8. Latin Quarter
9. Kongens Nytorv and Nyhavn
10. Slotsholmen

Dansk Design Centre

Preceding pages: **Marmorkirken and Amalienborg, seen from Amaliehaven.**

The Nimb building in Tivoli

1 Tivoli

Tivoli has virtually become synonymous with Copenhagen and should be high on the list for any visitor. Day or night, this park buzzes with the sounds of exhilarating rides. It is not only for adventure-seekers though. At night, the setting turns magical and romantic, with fairy lights and Japanese lanterns glowing in the darkness and music in the air *(see pp10–11)*.

2 Rådhuset

The Copenhagen Rådhus, or town hall, is a mock-Gothic building replete with fantastical sea creatures, built 1892–1905 and designed by architect Martin Nyrop. Its 105.6-m (346-ft) tower affords superb views of the city. Even if you don't want to do the full tour, you could pop in to see the pre-Raphaelitesque entrance way, or the Italianate reception hall. Many Copenhageners get married here, so you may just see several wedding parties on the steps. ◎ *Map H5 • Rådhuspladsen 1 • 33 66 33 66 • Open 7:45am–5pm Mon–Fri; Sat: open for tours only • Tours in English 3pm Mon–Fri, 10am Sat; Tower tour 11am & 2pm Mon–Fri, noon Sat*

3 Astronomical Clock

This ingenious clock, cased in a mahogany cabinet, was designed in 1872 by locksmith and watchmaker Jens Olsen. After waiting for 50 years to obtain funds, Olsen started working on the clock in 1943. He died two years later, but work continued and the clock was set in motion in 1955. Famous for its accuracy, this 14,000-part watch loses less than a second a century. It shows local time, solar time, sunrise and sunset times, sidereal time, celestial pole movement and the movement of the planets. ◎ *Map H5 • Rådhus, Rådhuspladsen 1 • 33 66 25 82 • Open 8:30am–4:30pm Mon–Fri, 10am–1pm Sat • Adm*

4 Ny Carlsberg Glyptotek

This superb art gallery is home to a fascinating collection of Mediterranean, Classical and Egyptian art and artifacts. Danish and 19th-century French works of art are also on display, including French Impressionist paintings. The museum is housed in a 19th-century building with a splendid cupola, beneath which lies an indoor winter garden, sculptures and water features. The modern wing is a wonderful, light-filled area *(see pp24–5)*.

Rådhus

5 Nationalmuseet

The National Museum is housed inside a former royal residence, dating from the 18th century. The exhibits trace Danish history, from ancient times to the present, including some amazing ethnographic collections. The most popular exhibits chart the history of Danes from the Ice Age to the Viking campaigns *(see pp26–7)*.

6 Dansk Design Center

The Dansk Design Center (DDC) is one of the city's most innovative exhibition organizers. It arranges shows with themes as diverse as Danish Design in Everyday Life to a DJ exhibition that allows visitors to create their own mix on turntables. Housed in a building designed by architect Henning Larsen, its intention is to showcase the use of design in business, while exhibiting Danish innovation. ◈ *Map H5 • HC Andersen Boulevard 27 • 33 69 33 69 • Open 10am–5pm Mon–Fri (to 9pm Wed), 11am–4pm Sat–Sun • Adm; free 5pm–9pm Wed; free daily for under-12s; free with Copenhagen Card • www.ddc.dk*

Vor Frue Kirke in the Latin Quarter

7 Amagertorv

This busy square is situated in the very middle of Strøget *(see p66)*. Note the attractive tiles that were designed by Bjørn Nørgaard. The square's focal point, the Storkespringvandet fountain (actually a heron) provided the inspiration for a Danish folk song of the 1960s, and today is a popular meeting place. The cafés Norden and Europa, found on either side of the square, are extremely popular ◈ *Map J4*

8 Latin Quarter

To the west of Strøget lies the Latin Quarter, the original home of the University of Copenhagen. It dates back to the Middle Ages when the primary language of culture and education was Latin. Some of the old university buildings are still in use, although much of the campus is now on the island of Amager. If you take a left off Strøget onto Nørregade, you will find the Universitetet and Vor Frue Kirke. Both have been used for their current purposes since the 15th and 13th centuries respectively; the current buildings, however, date back to the 19th century. The Rundetårn on Købmagergade is also worth a visit *(see pp16–17)*.

9 Kongens Nytorv and Nyhavn

At the top of Nyhavn stands the King's New Square (Kongens Nytorv), an elegant area surrounded by fashionable 18th-century mansions that now house banks, upmarket department stores and hotels. It is flanked by the Charlottenborg Slot (now an exhibition space and home to the academy of art) and the Royal Theatre (Det Kongelige

eatermuseet in Slotsholmen

Teater) *(see p18)*. Nyhavn (which
means "new harbour") is a
lively tourist area filled with
restaurants, cafés and old
sailing boats along the canal
quayside. The atmosphere here
is a stark contrast to what it
was in the 1670s, when sailors,
traders and low-lifes frequented
the area. Even until 40 years
ago, this was not a part of town
that many would have visited at
night. Urban regeneration has
changed all that and on sunny
evenings in particular, you may
not find a place to sit down
(see pp18–19).

10 Slotsholmen

A visit to Slotsholmen could
take up almost an entire day, as
there is plenty to see. Primarily
the site of Christiansborg Slot,
which burnt down in 1794, it is
now home to Denmark's
Parliament, and used by the
Queen for state functions (you
can visit the Royal Reception
Rooms on a guided tour). You
will find several museums here
as well for the tourist looking
for a bit of culture. The
delightful Theatre Museum
(Teatermuseet) *(see p35)* is
definitely worth a visit with the
main attraction being the
18th-century palace theatre.
Other sites include the palace
church and the 12th-century
ruins of the first Copenhagen
castle where its founder, Bishop
Absalon, resided *(see pp28–9)*.

Walking Tour

Morning

Start your day at the **Ny
Carlsberg Glyptotek**
(see p63); don't miss the
impressive Egyptian and
Impressionist collections.
Have an early lunch at the
charming **Winter Garden
Café** *(see pp24–5)*.

Afternoon

After lunch, cross HC
Andersen Boulevard and
visit the **Dansk Design
Center** or head to the
Nationalmuseet and take
one of the hour-long tours.
Then, stroll to the end of
Ny Vestergade until you
reach Frederiks Kanal.
Cross the bridge and visit
Christiansborg Slot *(see
p28)*. If you arrive by 2pm,
pop into the stables, the
Teatermuseet *(see p35)*
and the ruins before taking
a tour of the state rooms
at 3pm. Then, walk back
over the bridge and turn
right to Gammel Strand
(note the **Fishwife statue**,
see p37) for afternoon
snacks at one of the
restaurants and cafés.
Walk down Køb-
magergade via Højbro
Plads, right up to
Rundetårn *(see p16)*. If
you are feeling energetic,
hike to the top for a good
view of the city. Heading
back down, take a left
from Strøget and keep
walking until you reach
**Kongens Nytorv and
Nyhavn** – a perfect spot
for a relaxing evening
drink and supper at one
of the quayside bars and
restaurants. Instead of
heading back via Strøget,
take the less mainstream
Lille Strandstræde. Walk
to Rådhuspladsen and
go across to **Tivoli** *(see
p63)*. Spend the evening
at these lovely gardens
enjoying the atmosphere.

Left **Statue of HC Andersen** Centre **Caritas Springvandet** Right **A shop on Strøget**

Best of the Rest

1 Domhuset
The courthouse was built in 1805–15. The "Bridge of Sighs" across Slutterigade (prison street) was crossed by prisoners being led to trial. ⊗ *Map H4 • Nytorv 25 • Open 8:30am–4pm Mon–Thu (to 3pm Fri)*

2 Rådhuspladsen
On the south-western end of Strøget, the town hall square is one of the liveliest areas of the city. ⊗ *Map H5*

3 Statue of HC Andersen
This statue of the author by Henry Lukow-Nielsen dates from 1961. ⊗ *Map H5*

4 Caritas Springvandet
Dating back to 1608, the Charity Fountain is one of the oldest in the city. ⊗ *Map H4*

5 Guinness World Records Museum
This museum demonstrates 500 Guinness records. ⊗ *Map K4 • Østergade 16 • 33 32 31 31 • Open Sep–mid-Jun 10am–6pm daily (to 8pm Fri–Sat); mid-Jun–Aug 10am–10pm Sun–Thu • Adm; free with Copenhagen Card • www.guinness.dk*

6 Wonderful World of HC Andersen Museum
Scenes from Andersen's fairy tales and other memorabilia are found here. ⊗ *Map H5 • Rådhuspladsen 57 • 33 32 31 31 • Open Sep–mid-Jun 10am–6pm Sun–Thu, 10am–8pm Fri–Sat; mid-Jun–Aug 10am–10pm daily • Adm for adults; free with Copenhagen Card*

7 Post & Telemuseet
Located next to the main post office, this museum charts the history of communication from the 17th century onwards. ⊗ *Map J4 • Købmagergade 37 • 33 41 09 00 • Open 10am–5pm Tue–Sat (to 8pm Wed), noon–4pm Sun • Adm; free with Copenhagen Card • www.ptt-museum.dk*

8 Gammel Strand
This canalside street is home to excellent restaurants, one of the city's best flea markets, two art museums (Kunstforeningen Gl Strand and the Fotografisk Center) and is a pick-up point for DFDS Canal Tours (see p7). ⊗ *Map J4*

9 Georg Jensen Museum
The jewellery and homeware of the famous silversmith are on display here. ⊗ *Map J4 • Amagertorv 4 • 33 14 02 29 • Open 10am–6pm Mon–Thu, 10am–7pm Fri, 10am–5pm Sat (Jun–Sep Sun) • www.royalcopenhagen.com*

10 Strøget
This is the name given to the five main, interconnected shopping streets of Copenhagen. ⊗ *Map H5–K4*

iz Raz Sticks 'n' Veggies

Price Categories

For a three-course meal for one without alcohol, including taxes and extra charges.

⊗	up to Dkr200
⊗⊗	200–250
⊗⊗⊗	250–350
⊗⊗⊗⊗	350–450
⊗⊗⊗⊗⊗	over Dkr450

10 Dining

1 Riz Raz Sticks 'n' Veggies
Riz Raz is famous for its great value, Mediterranean-influenced vegetarian buffets, s well as meaty kebabs for he carnivorous. ◎ Map J5 • Kompagnistræde 20 • 33 15 05 75 • www.rizraz.dk • ⊗

2 L'Alsace
This gourmet restaurant pecializes in dishes from Alsace, with an emphasis on resh fish and seafood. ◎ Map K4 • Ny Østergade 9 • 33 14 57 43 • Closed Sun • www.alsace.dk • ⊗⊗⊗

3 Alberto K
One of the best restaurants n Denmark, Alberto K offers a blend of Scandinavian-Italian flavours. ◎ Map G5 • Radisson Blu Royal Hotel, 20th Floor, Hammerichsgade 1 • 33 42 61 61 • Closed Sun • Book ahead • www.alberto-k.dk • ⊗⊗⊗⊗⊗

4 A Porta eta 1792
Once the local eatery for HC Andersen, this café has been relaunched for a younger public. Offers both open sandwiches and French bistro food. Cocktails are also served. ◎ Map K4 • Kongens Nytorv 17 • 33 11 05 00 • Closed Sun • www.cafeaporta.dk • ⊗⊗⊗

5 St Gertrud's Kloster
Housed in a medieval convent, St Gertrud's serves mouth-watering Danish and European dishes in a candle-lit cavern. ◎ Map J4 • Hauser Plads 32 • 33 14 66 30 • www.sanktgertrudskloster.dk • ⊗⊗⊗⊗⊗

6 Thorvaldsens
This restaurant serves Nordic cuisine with a modern twist. ◎ Map J4 • Gammel Strand 34 • 33 32 04 00 • Open for lunch Sun Apr–Sep • www.thorvaldsens-hus.dk • ⊗⊗⊗

7 Atlas Bar
Exotic dishes served in a cool basement location. ◎ Map H4 • Larsbjørnsstræde 18 • 33 15 03 52 • Closed Sun • ⊗

8 Bankeråt
Enjoy steaks, salads and a selection of beers in this artistic venue. ◎ Map G3 • Ahlefeldtsgade 29 • 33 93 69 88 • www.bankeraat.dk • ⊗

9 Restaurant Peder Oxe
A well-established restaurant on a picturesque square. ◎ Map J4 • Gråbrødretov 11 • 33 11 00 77 • Open 11:30am–11pm daily • www.pederoxe.dk • ⊗⊗⊗

10 Husmanns Vinstue
This wine cellar/pub/restaurant offers many traditional herring-based dishes. ◎ Map H4 • Larsbjørns-stræde 2 • 33 11 58 86 • Closed Sun • www.husmannsvinstue.dk • ⊗⊗

Left **Birger Christensen** Centre **Illum Department Store** Right **Royal Copenhagen shop**

TOP 10 Strøget Shopping

Around Town – Tivoli North to Gothersgade

1 Illums Bolighus
This shrine to stylish interior design and kitchenware (mainly Italian and Danish) offers everything from Royal Copenhagen porcelain to groovy dog-biscuit dispensers and objects d'art. ✆ Map J4 • Amagertorv 10 • 33 14 19 41 • Open first Sun of the month • www.illumsbolighus.dk

2 Royal Copenhagen Porcelain
This flagship store offers a range of designs, from the classic 18th-century *flora danica* design to the modern and organic. ✆ Map J4 • Amagertorv 6 • 33 13 71 81 • Open Sun • www.royalcopenhagen.com

3 Illum Department Store
This stylish, six-storied department store offers quality clothing and homeware. There are also cafés, a bakery and a supermarket. ✆ Map K4 • Østergade 52 • 33 14 40 02 • Closed Sun • www.illum.eu

4 Birger Christensen
This exclusive fashion store sells Birger Christensen fur coats and jackets, as well as a wide collection of international labels. ✆ Map K4 • Østergade 38 • 33 11 55 55 • Closed Sun • www.birger-christensen.com

5 Georg Jensen
Georg Jensen's superb designs are available at the historic firm's flagship store, including stylish jewellery, watches, cutlery, candlesticks, antiques and even designer sunglasses. ✆ Map J4 • Amagertorv 4 • 33 11 40 80 • Closed Sun • www.georgjensen.com

6 Mads Nørgaard
Sells classic, casual Danish menswear, including the timeless trademark, unisex, striped top. ✆ Map J4 • Amagertov 15 • 33 32 01 39 • www.madsnorgaard.com

7 Noa Noa
Offers women's cottons, linens and silks in pretty styles and a similar collection for girls aged 3–12. ✆ Map K4 • Østergade 16 • 33 13 06 08 • Closed Sun • www.noa-noa.dk

8 Hay House
In addition to the store on Pilestræde, a larger branch has opened above Café Norden on Amagertov. Filled with bright plastic furniture and accessories. ✆ Map J4 • Østergade 61, 2nd Floor • 99 42 44 40 • Closed Sun • www.hay.dk

9 A Pair
Here you will find fashionable footwear for men and women, as well as leather bags and belts with large, silver buckles. ✆ Map K4 • Ny Østergade 3 • 33 91 99 20 • Closed Sun • www.apair.dk

10 Sand
This Danish fashion house offers a range of stylish and classic clothing and accessories for men and women. ✆ Map K4 • Østergade 40 • 33 14 21 21 • Closed Sun • www.sand-europe.com

 Strøget has no street sign: it's local for Frederiksberggade, Nygade, Vimmelskaftet, Amagertorv and Østergade combined.

Left **Sneaky Fox boutique** Right **Magasin du Nord**

10 Shops Off Strøget

Munthe Plus Simonsen
This award-winning Danish design duo offers wearable women's clothing and accessories with a stylish edge. ◎ Map K4 • Grønnegade 10 • 33 32 03 12 • www.muntheplussimonsen.com

Liebe
Fun ceramics in pretty pastel shades, all original designs by the owner, Susan Liebe. There are also gift ideas in the basement. ◎ Map J5 • Kompagnistræde 23 • 33 93 8 46 • Closed Sun • www.susanliebe.dk

Magasin du Nord
This is one of the city's oldest department stores, offering an upmarket selection of clothing and homeware. There is also a supermarket and plenty of places to eat. The discount sales held in January and late summer are very good. ◎ Map K4 • Kongens Nytorv 13 • 33 11 44 33 • Open first Sun of the month • www.magasin.dk

Sneaky Fox
This trendy women's boutique is especially well known for its variety of stockings, from the silly to the sophisticated. ◎ Map H4 • Studiestræde 25A • 33 91 25 20 • www.sneakyfox.dk

Fisk
Two floors of vintage clothing and ethnic gift ideas. Fisk also sells hand-made pieces by local artists and designers. There is a DanChurchAid café on-site. ◎ Map H4 • Sankt Peders Stræde 1 • 33 15 28 01

Grønlykke
Visit this funky shop if you are looking for colourful and kitsch household accessories, from kitchen bar stools to chandeliers. You will also find an assorted range of knick-knacks and bags. ◎ Map J4 • Lædderstræde 3–5 • 33 13 00 81 • www.gronlykke.com

Crème de la Crème à la Edgar
Lovely (though expensive) children's wear, toys and accessories are available here. ◎ Map J4 • Kompagnistræde 8 • 33 36 18 18 • www.cremedelacremealaedgar.dk

Akimbo
This is a great place for presents, especially for little girls, ranging from edible-looking candle cakes, to jewellery and kitsch toys. ◎ Map J4 • Hyskenstræde 3 • 33 11 13 01

Wettergren & Wettergren
Hidden away down a few steps leading to a basement, this charming shop sells vintage clothing and accessories with a modern twist. ◎ Map J4 • Lædderstræde 5 • 33 13 14 05

Stilleben
This tiny shop is filled with beautiful porcelain ceramics, available in a range of subtle colours, all created by young Danish potters and ceramic designers. ◎ Map J4 • Lædderstræde 14 • 33 91 11 31 • www.stilleben.dk

Left **Copenhagen Jazz House** Right **Nasa**

TOP 10 Nightlife

1 Studenterhuset
This charmingly grotty bar serves beer to students at discounted prices, and hosts local bands. ✪ *Map J3 • Købmagergade 52 • 35 32 38 61 • www.studenterhuset.com*

2 The Rock
Set in an old courthouse, this rock venue hosts great live rock shows. ✪ *Map H4 • Skindergade 45–47 • 33 91 39 13 • www.the-rock.dk*

3 Nasa
This club has top-notch DJs playing a mix from dance to modern soul with a twist. ✪ *Map K3 • Gothersgade 8F • 33 93 74 15 • Open midnight–6am Fri–Sat • www.nasa.dk*

4 Grand Teatret
This large, six-screen art house cinema has a smart, comfortable atmosphere and a small café. ✪ *Map H5 • Mikkel Bryggersgade 8 • 33 15 16 11 • www.grandteatret.dk*

5 The Lot
Located in the Galleri K complex next to Strøget, this restaurant transforms into a trendy, guestlist-only nightclub at weekends. ✪ *Map K4 • Pilestræde 12A • Open 11am–midnight Mon–Thu, 11am–3am Fri–Sat • Closed Sun*

6 Bar Rouge
This is one of the hippest cocktail bars in the city, with tastefully designed interiors. ✪ *Map H4 • In Hotel Skt Petri, Krystalgade 22 • 33 45 98 22 • www.hotelsktpetri.com*

7 Jazzhus Montmartre
This legendary jazz venue reopened in 2010. It may lack the underground feel nowadays, but still attracts world class jazz. ✪ *Map K3 • Store Regnegade 19A • 31 7, 34 94 • Café open noon–midnight Mon– Sat; concerts 8pm most nights • Book ahead • Adm • www.jazzhusmontmartre.d*

8 Copenhagen Jazz House
This live jazz venue attracts both international bands and home-grown talent. ✪ *Map J4 • Niels Hemmingsensgade 10 • 33 15 47 00 • www.jazzhouse.dk*

9 1105
The skilled bartenders at this hip cocktail bar mix some of the best drinks in the city. ✪ *Map K4 • Kristen Bernikows Gade 4 • 33 93 11 05 • Open 8pm–2am Wed, Thu & Sat, 4pm–2am Fri • Closed Sun– Tue • www.1105.dk*

10 Club Mambo
Dance to salsa in the club, or visit the lounge for some reggae and modern hits. ✪ *Map H5 • Vester Voldgade 85 • 33 11 97 66 • www.clubmambo.dk*

Price Categories

For a three-course	ⓢ up to Dkr200
meal for one	ⓢⓢ 200–250
without alcohol,	ⓢⓢⓢ 250–350
including taxes and	ⓢⓢⓢⓢ 350–450
extra charges.	ⓢⓢⓢⓢⓢ over Dkr450

Charlie's Bar

10 Historic Wining and Dining

1 Vandkunsten Sandwich Bar
This popular sandwich bar is housed in what was Copenhagen's oldest butcher's shop. ⓢ Map J5 • Rådhusstræde 17 • 33 13 90 40 • ⓢ

2 Skindbuksen
Founded in 1728, mariners, locals and tourists now rub shoulders at this unpretentious restaurant. ⓢ Map K4 • Lille Kongensgade 4 • 33 12 90 37 • Book ahead • www.skindbuksen.dk • ⓢⓢⓢ

3 Slotskælderen hos Gitte kik
This basement restaurant has changed little since opening in 1910. It is famous for its pickled herring and *schnapps*. ⓢ Map K4 • Fortunstræde 4 • 33 11 15 37 • Open 11am–3pm Tue–Sat (lunch only) • ⓢⓢ

4 Dan Turéll
One of the city's oldest cafés, it has a Parisian-style decor. ⓢ Map K3 • Store Regnegade 3–5 • 33 14 10 47 • www.danturell.dk • ⓢⓢⓢ

5 The Royal Café
This café has outdoor seating and a "smushi" menu, which combines traditional Danish smørrebrød with sushi. ⓢ Map J4 • Amagertorv 6 • 38 14 95 27 • www.theroyalcafe.dk • ⓢⓢ

6 Husmanns Vinstue
Once a stable, this comfortable, wood-panelled lunch venue serves tasty traditional Danish fare *(see p67).*

7 Hviids Vinstue
Copenhagen's oldest wine bar (established 1723), was one of HC Andersen's favourites. ⓢ Map K4 • Kongens Nytorv 19 • 33 15 10 64 • www.hviidsvinstue.dk

8 Charlie's Bar
Copenhagen's only Cask Marque pub, it serves 18 independent beers on tap. Danish breads are Hancock and Porse Guld. ⓢ Map J4 • Pilestræde 33 • 33 22 22 89 • www.charlies.dk

9 Perch's Tea Room
Not much seems to have changed since 1834, when AC Perch started importing fine teas. Weighed on scales, the tea is brewed with reverence. ⓢ Map J4 • Kronprinsensgade 5 • 33 15 35 77 • Closed Sun • www.perchs.dk

10 Café Petersborg
Established in 1746, this restaurant serves traditional Danish fare. ⓢ Map L2 • Bredgade 76 • 33 12 50 16 • Open 11:45am–4pm & 5–9pm Mon–Fri, 11:30am–4pm Sat • Closed Sun and hols • Book ahead • www.café-petersborg.dk • ⓢⓢ

Left **Rosenborg Slot** Right **Marmorkirken**

Nørrebro, Østerbro and North of Gothersgade

OF THESE THREE NEIGHBOURHOODS, *two are additions to the original Copenhagen site, which took up what is now called the "Inner City". Nørrebro, northeast of the Inner City, lies across the Dronning Louises Bro (Queen Louise's Bridge). Until the 19th century, this area was mainly farmland; today it is a lively, multicultural part of the city with plenty of bars, cafés and alternative shopping centres. Østerbro, slightly northeast of Nørrebro, has remained an uncluttered, suburban residential area since the 19th century. The train station, Østerport, was built in 1894–97 to help workers travel to the city centre, on the site of Copenhagen's fortified eastern gate. The area north of Gothersgade is part of the Inner City and takes in later parts of the original capital dating back to the Renaissance period.*

Frihedsmuseet

Sights

1. Assistens Kirkegård
2. Botanisk Have
3. Statens Museum for Kunst
4. Den Hirschsprungske Samling
5. Rosenborg Slot and Kongens Have
6. Davids Samling
7. Amalienborg
8. Marmorkirken
9. Kunstindustrimuseet
10. Frihedsmuseet

Preceding pages: **Christmas at Tivoli, the Chinese Pagoda.**

1 Assistens Kirkegård
If you are not a devoted fan of dead famous Danes, this cemetery may not be top of your list. However, it is a wonderful place to relax or take a romantic walk. The churchyard is beautiful and is located in the gritty Nørrebro district. ◈ Map C3 • Kapelvej • 35 37 19 17 • Open May–Aug 8am–8pm daily; Sep–Oct & Mar–Apr 8am–6pm daily; Nov–Feb 8am–4pm daily • www.assistens.dk

2 Botanisk Have
Among the prettiest outdoor spaces in the city, these gardens are studded with lakes, bridges and lovely flowerbeds. Climb the winding staircase for a great view of the exotic trees below. A geological and botanical museum are also here. ◈ Map H2–J2 • Gothersgade 130; Øster Farimagsgade 2C • 35 32 22 21 • Open May–Sep 8:30am–6pm daily; Oct–Apr 8:30am–4pm Tue–Sun • Closed Mon, 24 Dec & 1 Jan • www.botanic-garden.ku.dk

3 Statens Museum for Kunst
The National Gallery has an impressive collection of both national and international art, including works by the Old Masters and popular modern icons such as Matisse and Picasso (see pp22–3).

Statens Museum for Kunst

4 Den Hirschsprungske Samling
This small art museum is situated just behind the National Gallery and displays the collection of tobacco magnate, Heinrich Hirschsprung, given to the nation in 1902. Housed in a 19th-century building, the large collection is fittingly dedicated to 19th- and early 20th- century Danish art, including works by painters of the "Golden Age" and the Impressionistic Skagen School, whose signature style involved the use of bright colours and patchy brushwork. Contemporary furniture is also showcased at this museum. ◈ Map J1 • Stockholmsgade 20 • 35 42 03 36 • Open 11am–4pm Wed–Mon • Adm for adults; free Wed, free with Copenhagen Card • www.hirschsprung.dk

Botanisk Have

5 Rosenborg Slot and Kongens Have

Rosenborg Castle and King's Garden are among the city's highlights, especially on sunny days when the park is full of people and entertainment. Rosenborg Slot was built in 1606–34 on what was then the outskirts of the city. Today it is the only castle in the city centre that has not succumbed to fire. As a result, little has changed about the structure since the time the royal family inhabited it in the 17th and 18th centuries (see pp14–15).

6 Davids Samling

This museum holds the lovely private art collection that belonged to supreme court barrister and art lover, CL David. The superb Islamic collection is the largest in Scandinavia, and includes a fine range of Islamic art and artifacts from the 8th to the 19th centuries. There is also a collection of European decorative arts from the 18th and 19th centuries. Set in an elegant, 19th-century town house, it is interesting to see the exhibits in a contemporaneous setting. ⊛ Map K3 • Kronprinsessegade 30–32 • 33 73 49 49 • Open 1–5pm Tue & Fri–Sun, 10am–5pm Wed–Thu • Closed Mon • Adm free • www.davidmus.dk

7 Amalienborg

If you wish to look around inside the royal palaces, you need to visit on a weekend in summer. If you are unable to do so, you can only visit certain parts of the palace that have been set up as a museum. Either way, the Amalienborg complex is worth looking at from the outside. The palaces were built as an important part of the 18th-century aristocratic district Frederiksstaden and are very different from the narrow streets and houses of the old quarter. When it was first built, it was visually linked to the Marble Church (see below); the modern Opera House (see p8) and the construction across the harbour on Holmen offer a contemporary visual contrast (see pp20–21).

8 Marmorkirken

Standing close to the Amalienborg is the splendid Marmorkirken (Marble Church), a part of the great architectural design for the Frederiksstad area. However, plans for its construction were so extravagant that finances ran out and work was abandoned in 1770. For more than a century it stood as a picturesque ruin before being rescued and financed by a Danish industrialist. It

Amalienborg

Kunstindustrimuseet

was in 1894 that the church was finally completed *(see pp20–21)*.

9 Kunstindustrimuseet

The National Museum of Art and Design is housed in a magnificent 18th-century Rococo building that was formally Denmark's first hospital. The collection comprises everything from Danish-designed colanders and cardboard chairs to posters, textiles and Chinese decorative arts. The garden, Grønnegard, has its own summer theatre. Buy a picnic basket from the museum café to eat under the linden trees. ⊗ *Map L2 • Bredgade 68 • 33 18 56 56 • Open 11am–5pm Tue–Sun • Adm for adults; free with Copenhagen Card • www.kunstindustrimuseet.dk*

10 Frihedsmuseet

The Danish Resistance Museum pays tribute to, and tells the stories of, the people who lived in Denmark during the German occupation (1940–45). It explores their daily lives and the resistance activities that they upheld – from underground newspapers and radio stations to sabotage and the rescue of virtually every Jew in Denmark from under the noses of the Germans. ⊗ *Map L2 • Churchill-parken 7 • 33 47 39 21 • Open May–Sep 10am–5pm Tue–Sun; Oct–Apr 10am–3pm Tue–Sun • www.natmus.dk*

Walking Tour

Morning

Start your day at the **Den Hirschsprungske Samling** *(see p75)* museum, amongst the Skagen School's Danish Impressionist paintings. Then cross the gardens to the impressive **Statens Museum for Kunst** *(see 75)*; take an audio guide to learn about the displays.

Afternoon

For lunch, stop over at either the museum café or the **Botanisk Have** *(see p75)* café, depending upon the weather. The gardens are a great place for a picnic, too. Don't forget to visit the palm house. Heading out from the gate on Øster Voldgade, cross over to **Rosenborg Slot.** You can spend a few enjoyable hours here, visiting the castle, the crown jewels and strolling through the gardens. Then, leave from the Kronprinsessegade gate and pop into the **Davids Samling** museum for some Islamic art. Walk down Dronningens Tværgade, take a left onto Bredgade and walk right up to **Marmorkirken**. If you are here by 3pm, take a tour up to the tower. Right in front of the church is the **Amalienborg Palace Square**. Take a walk through it to the pretty banks of the harbour and see the **Opera House** *(see p8)* across the water. If you are up for a 20-minute walk, head toward the **Little Mermaid** *(see p78)*, passing the distinctive **Gefionspringvandet** *(see p78)* and **Frihedsmuseet** (worth a visit). To get back to town, hop on to the No 26 bus from Folke Bernadottes Allé.

Left **Gefionspringvandet** Right **Kastellet**

TOP 10 Best of the Rest

1 Gefionspringvandet
A dramatic sight, this bronze statue represents the tale of goddess Gefion ploughing enough land to create the island of Zealand (see p37). ✪ Map M2

2 Medicinsk Museion
The Medical Museum of Copenhagen University has exhibits (some gruesome) dating back to the 18th century. ✪ Map L2 • Bredgade 62 • 35 32 38 00 • Open 1–5pm Wed–Fri & Sun • Guided tour in English 2:30pm Jul–Aug • Adm for adults • www.mhm.ku.dk

3 Little Mermaid (Den Lille Havfrue)
This statue of the heroine of Andersen's fairy tale, The Little Mermaid, perched on a rock in the harbour, has been staring out to sea since 1913. ✪ Map M1 • Langelinie

4 Amaliehaven
Filled with box hedges and fountains, this modern park lies to the east of Amalienborg, facing the harbour with views of the Opera House (see p20).

5 Kastellet
This pentagram-shaped fortress was built as protection against the Swedes, but only ever used against the English in 1807. ✪ Map L1 • 33 47 95 00 • Only grounds open to visitors

6 Kastelskirken
This military church at Kastellet has been holding services since the 17th century. ✪ Map L1 • Kastellet • 33 15 65 58 • Open 9am–1pm Mon–Thu, 10am–noon Fri • Regular free concerts 2pm Sun

7 St Albans Kirke
Named after St Alban, England's first martyr, Denmark's onl Anglican church is a Neo-Gothic building from 1885. ✪ Map M2 • Churchillparken • 39 62 77 36 • Service 10:30am Sun & Wed • www.st-albans.dk

8 Kongelige Afstøbningssamling
The Royal Cast Collection is heralded on the walk along the harbour with a replica of Michelangelo's statue of David. ✪ Map M • Toldbodgade 40 • 33 74 85 75 • Open 2–4pm Tue, 2–8pm Wed, 2–5pm Sun • Free guided tours 3pm Sun (in Danish)

9 Alexander Nevsky Kirke
This Russian orthodox church (1883) was a gift from Tsar Alexander III to celebrate his marriag to the Danish Princes Marie Dagmar. ✪ Map L3 • Bredgade 53 • 33 13 60 46 • Open 11:30am–1:30pm

10 Fælledparken
Copenhagen's largest park is where the city gathers for the annual 1st May celebrations. ✪ Map D.

Around Town – Nørrebro, Østerbro and North of Gothersgade

Restaurant Zeleste

Price Categories

For a three-course meal for one without alcohol, including taxes and extra charges.

® up to Dkr200
®® 200–250
®®® 250–350
®®®® 350–450
®®®®® over Dkr450

⑩ Restaurants and Cafés

1 Restaurant Zeleste
This charming restaurant with a cosy interior serves good Continental-Danish fusion food. ® Map L4 • Store Strandstræde 6 • 33 16 06 06 • www.zeleste.dk • ®®®

2 Ida Davidsen
Excellent smørrebrød (open sandwiches) are on offer here, with an array of toppings. ® Map K3 • Store Kongensgade 70 • 33 91 36 55 • Open for lunch only • Closed Sat–Sun & Jul • www.idadavidsen.dk • ®®®

3 Salt Bar and Restaurant
Set inside an airy, 18th-century granary, this elegant bar and restaurant serves cocktails and French-Danish cuisine. ® Map J3 • Toldbodgade 24–28 • 33 74 14 44 • www.saltrestaurant.dk • ®®®®

4 Café Oscar
A conservative café that has retained its classic decor over the decades. ® Map L3 • Bredgade 58 • 33 12 50 10 • Open 9:30am–11pm daily • www.cafeoscar.dk • ®®®

5 Pussy Galore's Flying Circus
Stop at this trendy café-bar for burgers, sandwiches or salads. ® Map D3 • Skt Hans Torv 30, Nørrebro • 35 24 53 00 • www.pussy-galore.dk • ®

6 Taverna Philoxenia
This bright, airy taverna serves quality Greek dishes at reasonable prices. ® Map D3 • Ravnsborggade 16B • 35 36 36 40 • Open 4–10pm Mon–Sat • www.philoxenia.dk • ®®

7 Teatime
This English-inspired basement-café offers sandwiches, cakes and sweets, and serves tea in elegant porcelain cups. ® Map C3 • Birkegade 3, Nørrebro • 35 35 50 58 • Afternoon Tea 2:30–5pm • www.teatime.dk • ®

8 Bopa
Have a hearty brunch or café lunch (burgers, moussaka, etc.), and cocktails in the evening. ® Map E1 • Bopa Plads, Løgstørgade 8 • 35 43 05 66 • www.cafebopa.dk • ®

9 Fischer
Formerly a pub, this tiny Italian restaurant has retained much of the original design. It is a favourite with local restaurant critics. Reservations necessary. ® Map E2 • Victor Borges Plads 12 • 35 42 39 64 • Open 11am–midnight daily • ®®®

10 Kate's Joint
This popular eatery offers cheap dishes with South American, Indonesian and Caribbean influences. ® Map C4 • Blågårdsgade 12 • 35 37 44 96 • Open 5:30–10pm daily; also 11am–3:30pm Thu–Sun • ®

Left **Eco Ego** Right **Tage Andersen Boutique & Galleri**

TOP 10 Shopping

1 Tage Andersen Boutique & Galleri

Run by flower artist and designer Tage Andersen, this flower shop, gallery and museum is full of lovely and unique arrangements. ⓢ *Map K4 • Ny Adelgade 12 • 33 93 09 13 • www.tage-andersen.com*

2 Marie Skellingsted

Here you will find an eclectic mix of designer and vintage items, including designer wear, jewellery, bags, home accessories and kitsch items for kids. ⓢ *Map L3 • Bredgade 4 • 33 11 49 50 • www.marieskellingsted.dk*

3 Susanne Juul

This establishment supplies hats to celebrities and royalty. ⓢ *Map K3 • Store Kongensgade 14 • 33 32 25 28 • www.susannejuul.dk*

4 Normann Copenhagen

This vast warehouse housed in an old cinema is filled with designer furniture, clothes and interior design items, including the company's own lines. ⓢ *Map E2 • Østerbrogade 70 • 35 55 44 59*

5 Eco Ego

Denmark's first fair trade, organic lifestyle shop sells everything, from shoes and skincare products to games. ⓢ *Map H3 • Nørre Farimagsgade 82 • 32 12 06 12*

6 Baan Suan

Visit this store for pretty, feminine clothing with embroidery, flower motifs and polka dots. Do also check out their varied range of colourful, ethnic jewellery, sunglasses and bags. ⓢ *Map C3 • Elmegade 18 • 35 39 19 40*

7 Nyhavns Glaspusteri

This charming glass gallery is where glassblower Christian Edwards sculpts and sells his creations. ⓢ *Map L4 • Toldbodgade 4 • 33 13 01 34 • www.copenhagenglass.d*

8 Phenix

You will find antique pieces ranging from furniture and paintings to silverware and glass items. ⓢ *Map D3 • Ravnsborggade 16A • 35 37 55 33 • www.phenixx.dk*

9 Juice

This was one of the first trendy clothing boutiques to be set up in Nørrebro. ⓢ *Map C3 • Elmegade 17 • 35 36 15 58*

10 Glam

High-end vintage pieces are available at this second-hand store. The 1960s and 1970s collection is especially good. ⓢ *Map C3 • Silkegade 7, Nørrebro • 35 38 50 41 • www.glam.dk*

Left **Rust** Right **Gefährlich**

🔟 Nightlife

1 Props Coffee Shop
The low ceilings and relaxed ambience of this Berlin-inspired bar make it the perfect place to enjoy fine, locally brewed beer. ⬥ *Map C3* • *Blågårdsgade 5* • *35 36 99 55*

2 Gefährlich
Despite an unimpressive decor, this is one of the most popular bars in the area. It also has a good restaurant and live music. ⬥ *Map C3* • *Fælledvej 7* • *35 24 16 00* • *Closed Mon* • *www.gefahrlich.dk*

3 Rust
Tune into Copenhagen's alternative music scene live at this trendy bar. There is a nightclub in the basement. ⬥ *Map C3* • *Guldbergsgade 8* • *35 24 52 00* • *Nightclub: Min age Wed–Thu 18, Fri–Sat 20* • *www.rust.dk*

4 Café Pavillonen
Located beside a lake, this lovely, 18th-century-style rotunda holds open-air salsa with DJs in summer. ⬥ *Map D2* • *Borgmester Jensens Allé 45, Østerbro* • *35 38 73 83* • *Open Apr–Oct* • *www.cafepavillonen.dk*

5 Empire Bio Cinema
This comfortable arts cinema holds good programmes and has a cosy bar and café area. ⬥ *Map C3* • *Guldbergsgade 29F* • *35 36 00 36* • *www.empirebio.dk*

6 Bodega
Popular and reasonably priced, this pre-clubbing venue serves good bar food. It also has a dance floor; DJ sessions are held on Fridays and Saturdays and kick in at 10pm. ⬥ *Map C4* • *Kapelvej 1* • *35 39 07 07* • *www.bodega.dk*

7 Park Diskotek
This black-walled, pink-curtained club specializes in R&B and house music. Brunch is available in the adjoining café. ⬥ *Map E2* • *Østerbrogade 79* • *70 33 32 32* • *Min age: 20 (Fri), 23 (Sat)* • *www.parkcafe.dk*

8 Pussy Galore's Flying Circus
A hangout for Crown Prince Frederik in his bachelor days, this trendy club serves hamburgers, salads and cocktails (see p79).

9 The Oak Room
This tiny cocktail bar consists of one long narrow room. Popular with the locals. ⬥ *Map C3* • *Birkegade 10* • *38 60 38 60* • *www.oakroom.dk*

10 Mexibar
This cosy, Mexican-inspired bar serves good cocktails. The staff are friendly, too. ⬥ *Map C3* • *Elmegade 27* • *35 37 77 66*

Left **Frederiksberg Slot** Right **Zoo**

Vesterbro and Frederiksberg

VESTERBRO AND FREDERIKSBERG *lie side by side to the south-west and west of the Inner City. In the 19th century both Vesterbro and Frederiksberg were outside the city walls; this was when Tivoli was built on Vesterbro's extreme edge. Vesterbro was formally an area where the poor lived in humble two-room flats with no running water and included a red-light district. Although the area retains an edginess shared only by the Nørrebro district, much of it has been regenerated. Today, you will find a thriving underground culture, designer fashion outlets and a multicultural population. In contrast, Frederiksberg was a green, prosperous country village that became increasingly popular as the upper and middle classes began to revel in the countryside in the 18th century. It is now a tranquil, upmarket residential area, and remains an independent municipality that is not officially a part of Copenhagen.*

Sights

1. Københavns Museum
2. Frederiksberg Have
3. Zoologisk Have
4. Radisson Blu Royal Hotel
5. Carlsberg Museum and Visitor Centre
6. Frederiksberg Slot
7. Tycho Brahe Planetarium
8. Storm P Museet
9. Bakkehusmuseet
10. Cisternerne – Museet for Moderne Glaskunst

Storm P Museet

Københavns Museum

The City Museum takes you on a journey through the city's history, right from its small beginnings on the island of Slotsholmen in the 12th century. There are many interesting exhibits, including atmospheric reconstructions, a slide show of Copenhagen through the ages and sights of a medieval town. Outside the building, the large model of medieval Copenhagen gives a clear view of the buildings that existed then and the area that was covered by the city.
◈ Map C5 • Vesterbrogade 59 • 33 21 07 72 • Open 10am–5pm daily • Adm for adults; Fri free • www.bymuseum.dk

Frederiksberg Have

Frederiksberg Gardens surround Frederiksberg Slot (see p84) and make up a lovely green area that recalls the castle's aristocratic past. The park was designed (1798–1802) to conform with the Romantic style of the English garden. Several buildings here date back to the Golden Age (1800–50), including the Chinese Pavilion, the Neo-Classical Møstings House, the Swiss House (a cottage built for the royal family to have tea) and the colonnaded Apis Temple.
◈ Map A5 • Open 6am–sundown daily

Frederiksberg Have

Zoologisk Have

Open 365 days a year, this zoo makes for a lovely day out. Here you will find a variety of animals like tigers and monkeys (including the tiny, endangered Golden Lion Tamarins). Visit the Norman Foster-designed elephant house, where two large domes in the roof flood the stables with daylight, providing a great place to see these magnificent creatures.
◈ Map A5 • Roskildevej 32 • 72 20 02 00 • Open Nov–Feb 10am–4pm daily; Mar 10am–4pm Mon–Fri, 10am–5pm Sat–Sun; Apr–May, Sep 10am–5pm Mon–Fri, 10am–6pm Sat–Sun; Jun 10am–6pm daily; Jul–Aug 10am–9pm daily • Adm • www.zoo.dk

Radisson Blu Royal Hotel

The city's tallest building, this 20-storey tower-block hotel, designed by architect Arne Jacobsen (right down to the cutlery), represents the cutting-edge design of the 1950s. About the radical design, Arne Jacobsen said, "They call it the 'punch card', and it's funny, because that is what it looks like when the windows are open on a hot summer's day." ◈ Map G5 • Hammerichsgade 1 • 33 42 60 00 • www.radisson.com

Københavns Museum

Carlsberg Brewery

Carlsberg Museum and Visitor Centre

The Carlsberg Brewery, established by Jacob Jacobsen in 1847, hosts an exhibition charting the brewery's history and its brands (including a collection of 13,000 of the 16,000 Carlsberg bottle and label designs). The tour takes you to the old, cobble-stoned premises and the stable of dray horses, and finishes in the Carlsberg bar, where free beers (or soft drinks) await you. Make sure to visit the tiled Dipylon Gate (1892) and the Elephant Gate (1901) at the second brewery established in 1889 by Jacob Jacobsen's son, Carl. ⊗ Map A6 • Gamle Carlsberg Vej 11 • 33 27 12 82 • Open May–Aug 10am–5pm Tue–Sun (to 7:30pm Thu); Sep–Apr 10am–4pm Tue–Sun • Adm • www.visitcarlsberg.dk

Frederiksberg Slot

Not to be mistaken for Frederiksborg Slot in Hillerød (see p98), this castle was originally a 17th-century pavilion built by Frederik IV as a royal court. As it was rather small, it was extended several times since its construction. The building that stands here today (built in 1829) has an Italianate, Baroque architecture and is used as a training school for army cadets. ⊗ Map A5 • Closed to the public

Tycho Brahe Planetarium

The permanent exhibition at the Planetarium includes display on the natural sciences, astronomy and space travel. However, one of the biggest attractions is the IMAX cinema; visitors are blown away by the enormous, high-quality images on the 1,000-sq-m (over 10,500-sq-ft) dome screen. Films cover topics like astronomy and space research and virtually transport you to another world. ⊗ Map C5 • Gammel Kongevej 10 • 33 12 12 24 • Open 11:30am–9pm Mon 9:30am–9pm Tue–Sun • Adm (includes exhibition and film showing) • Min age for films: 3 yrs • www.tycho.dk

Storm P Museet

This small museum is a delightful find. It is dedicated to the whimsical and satirical wit of the Danish cartoonist Storm P, whose distinctive style seems to recall the social realism of the late 19th and early 20th centuries such as the styles of Daumier, Toulouse Lautrec and Degas. His sense of humour comes through brilliantly in the dialogues of his characters. If you speak Danish, you will derive great enjoyment from these cartoons. However, non-Danish speakers will also enjoy the displays visually. ⊗ Map A5 • Frederiksberg Runddel • 38 86 05 23 • Open May–Sep 10am–4pm daily; Oct–Apr 10am–4pm Wed, Sat & Sun • Adm for adults • www.stormp-museet.dk

Bakkehusmuseet

Formerly, the home of 19th-century, Golden Age literary personalities, Kamma and Lyhne Rahbek, this old house is now a cultural museum. Four rooms have retained their original decor (1802–30), and two are dedicated to the Danish poets Johannes Ewald and Adam Oehlenschläger.

If the Carlsberg Brewery has given you a taste for beer, head for Charlie's Bar, see p71; for microbreweries, see p53.

Jacob Jacobsen

Lager beer was unheard of in Copenhagen until news arrived of "Bavarian beers" being made by ageing (lagering). Jacob Jacobsen (1811–87), who made beer in the ale-making tradition, left at once for Munich to get some lager yeast. In 1847, he introduced his first lager and set up the Carlsberg Brewery (named after his son). Carlsberg lager is now among the world's best.

You will also find a variety of HC Andersen memorabilia here.
🟤 Map B6 • Rahbeks Allé 23, Frederiks-
berg • 33 31 43 62 • Open 11am–4pm
Tue–Sun • Adm; free with Copenhagen
Card • www.bakkehusmuseet.dk

Cisternerne – Museet for Moderne Glaskunst

This remarkable, candle-lit glass museum is intriguing not only for its stained glass exhibits by artists like Per Kirkeby and Robert Jacobsen, but also for its location. Set inside the cave-like water cistern of an old supply plant, it lies beneath the grassy lawns of Frederiksberg Have and has numerous thin stalactites on the ceiling.
🟤 Map A6 • Søndermarken, Roskildevej
5 • 33 21 93 10 • Open Mar–Oct
2–6pm Thu–Fri; Feb & Nov 2–5pm Mon–
Fri, 11am–5pm Sat–Sun & hols • Closed
Dec–Jan • Adm; free for under-14s
• www.cisternerne.dk

Tycho Brahe Planetarium

A Walk Around Vesterbro

🕐 Start at the central station, Hovedbanegård, and see the *Frihedsstøtten* or "pillar of freedom" (1792). Continue down Vesterbrogade and take a left on Reventlowsgade and then a right on to Istedgade till you arrive at the old red light district. Then, walk up to **Halmtorvet**; once a cattle market, it is now filled with cafés and restaurants. The large building directly opposite is the **Øksnehallen**, Vesterbro's biggest cultural exhibition space. Take a right on Skydebanegade, where you will see houses dating back to the 19th century. At the end of this area is a wall (1887) that protected inhabitants from shooting practice that took place in the gardens on the other side. Go through the gate in the wall, through the park, to the **Københavns Museum** *(see p83)*. Take a look at the city model outside and, if you wish, visit the museum. Continue along Vesterbrogade, taking a left onto Oehlenschlæg-ersgade, where you will find an extraordinary mosaic-covered bar that was put together by the late Nigerian-born artist, Manuel Tafat. Head back to Vesterbrogade for lunch at **Les Trois Cochons** *(see p87)* on Værnedamsvej, or continue down Oehlen-schlægersgade until you reach the trendy bars and boutiques on Istedgade. You could also stop over for lunch at **Café Bang & Jensen** at 130 or just enjoy a nice cup of coffee at **Riccos** at 119 *(see p86)*. Spend the rest of the afternoon browsing through the stylish shops.

Left **Designer Zoo** Right **Emmerys Bakery**

Shopping

1 Kusine Bodil og Vildbassen

This funky kids' store offers every-thing from Osh Kosh dungarees and Katvig denim dresses to flamingo umbrellas, toddler-sized kitchens and retro games. ✎ *Map B6 • Enghave Plads 10 • 33 24 28 84*

2 Donn Ya Doll

Donn Ya Doll opened in the techno-era '90s and has retained something of a space age look. It stocks hip and original clothing, and accessories, some designed by the shop's owner. ✎ *Map C5 • Istedgade 55 • 33 22 66 35*

3 Girlie Hurly

This shop is filled with quirky, colourful items for girls, from bags and candles to lamps and crockery. ✎ *Map C6 • Istedgade 99 • 33 24 22 41*

4 Rockahula

This intriguing little boutique is dedicated to all things '50s and rockabilly, including a children's line. ✎ *Map C6 • Istedgade 91 • 26 23 42 67 • www.rockahula.dk*

5 Gustus

You will find fabulous, rea-sonably priced glass items at this shop, run by a Polish glassmaker. There are also ceramics and jewellery. ✎ *Map C6 • Istedgade 67B • 35 83 60 68 • www.gustus.dk*

6 Tiger Lily

This tiny vintage clothes shop sells funky, designer second-hand clothes in retro Bohemian styles. ✎ *Map C5 • Værnedamsvej 11 • 44 61 22 04 • Closed Mon*

7 Designer Zoo

This is a mecca for the design conscious, with clothing, ceramics, jewellery and even furniture by in-house designers. ✎ *Map B5 • Vesterbrogade 137 • 33 24 94 93 • www.dzoo.dk*

8 Emmerys Bakery

Visit this excellent gourmet store for tasty organic goodies, including breads, patisseries, chocolates, pasta, wine and cheese. ✎ *Map C5 • Vesterbrogade 34 • 33 22 77 63 • Open Sundays • www.emmerys.dk*

9 Værnedamsvej

This gourmet food street, nicknamed Little Paris, has butchers, fish-mongers, wine and chocolate shops. ✎ *Map C5*

10 Le Marché Deli Takeaway

Stop here for home-cooked, take-away meals. Changing evening menu. ✎ *Map C5 • Værnedamsvej 2 • www.cofoco.dk*

Café Lindevang

🔟 Dining

Café Lindevang
Café Lindevang is known for their generous portions. Meatballs and herring are accompanied by a range of *schnapps*. ◎ Map C5 • Sløjfen 6 (Lindevang metro stop) • 38 34 38 34 • Closed Sun • www. cafelindevang.dk • ⊛⊛

Café Bang & Jensen
This ex-pharmacy is now a popular café-bar. Fun cocktails and good music make for lively nights. ◎ Map C6 • Istedgade 130 • 33 25 53 18 • www.bangogjensen.dk • ⊛

Les Trois Cochons
Aptly named ("the three pigs" in French), this restaurant is inside an old butcher's shop. It serves great southern French food at reasonable prices. ◎ Map C5 • Værnedamsvej 10 • 33 31 70 55 • Book ahead • ⊛⊛⊛

Cofoco
Delicious, reasonably priced French-Danish food is served at a long communal table. ◎ Map C5 • Abel Cathrines Gade 7 • 33 13 60 60 • Closed Sun • Book ahead • ⊛⊛⊛

Sticks 'n' Sushi
Try the mouthwatering sushi, sashimi or yakitori at this friendly Euro-Japanese café-bar. ◎ Map C6 • Istedgade 62 • 33 23 73 04 • www.sushi.dk • ⊛

Famo
Co-owned by the former head chef of Era Ora (see p48), this restaurant serves inexpensive, good quality Italian cuisine. ◎ Map C5 • Saxogade 3 • 33 23 22 50 • Book ahead • www.famo.dk • ⊛⊛⊛⊛

Frederiks Have
A former pub, this 19th-century building, close to Frederiksberg, Have offers outside dining in a covered courtyard. It serves Swedish-Danish specialities. ◎ Map A4 • Smallegade 41 • 38 88 33 55 • Closed Sun • www.frederikshave.dk • ⊛⊛⊛⊛

Riccos
The aroma of fresh coffee wafting from this café is hard to resist. ◎ Map C6 • Istedgade 119 • 33 31 04 40 • www.riccos.dk • ⊛

Formel B
Enjoy French-influenced food made with farm-fresh ingredients on the terrace, or in the candle-lit interiors. ◎ Map B5 • Vesterbrogade 182 • 33 25 10 66 • Closed Sun–Mon • Book ahead • www.formel-b.dk • ⊛⊛⊛⊛⊛

Restaurant Klubben
This pub is famous for its large portions of Danish food. ◎ Map B5 • Enghavevej 4 • 33 31 40 15 • ⊛

Price Categories

For a three-course meal for one without alcohol, including taxes and extra charges.	⊛ up to Dkr200
	⊛⊛ 200–250
	⊛⊛⊛ 250–350
	⊛⊛⊛⊛ 350–450
	⊛⊛⊛⊛⊛ over Dkr450

Left **Christiania** Right **Overgaden Neden Vandet**

Christianshavn and Holmen

AFTER THE INNER CITY, *this settlement on the island of Amager is the oldest part of Copenhagen. There is some evidence that it was inhabited during the Stone Age. In 1521, Christian II invited Dutch gardeners (whom he held in high regard) to this fertile area to plant and run market gardens. A century later, Christian IV built fortifications in the area and a town on an island at the north end. Soon, the Amagerbro bridge was built to connect the two islands; the Knippelsbro bridge stands in its place today. The canals of Christianshavn, lined with houseboats and pretty 17th-century houses, are a special attraction in this charming area that is reminiscent of Amsterdam. Holmen, to the north of Christianshavn, is made up of three man-made islets. It was created in 1690 as a naval area with dockyards, accommodation and*

offices; the navy remained here until 1989. Since then, the area has seen an increase in public spaces, forums, residential housing, art and design schools, and now also includes the impressive Opera House.

Operaen

🔟 Sights

1. Christiania
2. Christians Kirke
3. Vor Frelsers Kirke
4. Inderhavnen
5. Harbour Tours
6. Overgaden Neden Vandet & Overgaden Oven Vandet
7. North Atlantic House
8. Orlogsmuseet
9. Operaen
10. Gammel Dok

Christiania

In the 1970s, this rebellious squatters' enclave, set up in abandoned military barracks, was an inspirational new society with its own set of laws, readily available drugs and no tax system. The area has now become a bit more conventional; the inhabitants have been paying taxes since 1994, and the stands that sold drugs on Pusher Street closed down in 2004. However, relations between Christiania and the Danish authorities have never been friendly and the area's status is still in doubt. There are no actual sights but many hippy hangouts. ◎ Map M5

Christians Kirke

Originally known as Frederiks Kirke, this interesting, yellow-brick church was renamed as Christians Kirke (after Christian IV, founder of this part of Copenhagen) in 1901. It was built between 1755–59 in the Rococo style by Nicolai Eigtved, Frederik V's master architect. The interior looks almost like a theatre, with second-level seating galleries and the altar taking the place of the stage. The elegant tower was added by Eigtved's son-in-law, GD Anthon, 10 years after the church was built. ◎ Map K6 • Strandgade 1 • 32 54 15 76 • Open Mar–Oct 8am–6pm daily; Nov–Feb 8am–5pm daily

Vor Frelsers Kirke

This magnificent Baroque church was built (1682–96) by the Dutch-Norwegian architect Lambert van Haven in the form of a Greek cross. Its trademark twisted tower was added 50 years later (1749–52). Inside the church is bright and well-lit, thanks to its white walls and large windows. Look out for the

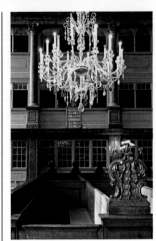

Christians Kirke

putti-covered font, presented in 1702 by Frederik IV's morganatic wife who hoped to have children. Unfortunately, she died in 1704 during childbirth and the baby died nine months later. Don't miss the marvellous altarpiece, which represents God as the Sun and depicts the scene in the garden of Gethsemane, when Christ prayed that he should not die on the cross. The organ, built like a three-storey house, rests on two elephants. ◎ Map L6
• Sankt Annae Gade 29 • 32 54 68 83
• Open Apr–Aug 11am–4:30pm Mon–Sat, noon–4:30pm Sun; Sep–Mar 11am–3:30pm Mon–Sat, noon–3:30pm Sun • Tower: Open Apr–Jun & mid-Sep–Oct 11am–4pm daily; Jul–mid-Sep 11am–7pm daily • Adm for tower • www.vorfrelserskirke.dk

Inderhavnen

You simply cannot ignore the water in Christianshavn. Its canals are tributaries of the Inner Harbour (Inderhavnen), which separates it from the rest of the city. The harbour widens further up the coast to become the Sound (Øresund). ◎ Map J6–M4

Orlogsmuseet

Harbour Tours
5 A harbour tour, which usually starts from Nyhavn *(see p8)*, is a great way to see Copenhagen. It will take you through the canals of Christianshavn. From the water you can appreciate the maritime nature of the city and get a sense of how it developed over the centuries. ◉ *Map L4*

Overgaden Neden Vandet & Overgaden Oven Vandet
6 These two cobbled streets lie on opposite sides of the Christianshavn canal. Overgaden Neden Vandet (which means "upper street below the water") is the quayside that runs along the Sound side of the canal. It is lined with 17th-century buildings, one of which is the Era Ora restaurant *(see p93)*. Overgaden Oven Vandet ("upper street above the water") is also lined with 17th-century houses, including the Royal Danish Naval Museum *(see opposite)*. ◉ *Map L6–M5*

North Atlantic House
7 The North Atlantic House is a cultural centre for the nations of Iceland, Greenland and the Faroes. Housed in an 18th-century warehouse, formerly the Greenlandic

Trading Square that hosts art displays and events. The Noma restaurant is also based here *(see pp49 & 93)*. ◉ *Map M4 • Strandgade 91 • 32 83 37 00 • Open 10am–5pm Mon–Fri, noon–5pm Sat–Sun • Adm (free for under-11s) • www.bryggen.dk*

Orlogsmuseet
8 The Royal Danish Naval Museum, located in the area that was influenced by the navy and its docks for centuries, document Danish naval history from 1669. There are beautiful, detailed models of ships and harbours, and a few reconstructions of important Danish sea battles. Some of the models were used as sailors' teaching aids, to show cadets how to strip and re-rig the sails. Most of the information is available in both Danish and English. The museum building (dating back to 1781) was originally used as a naval hospital and then as a state prison until the 1830s. ◉ *Map L5 • Overgaden Oven Vandet 58 • 33 11 60 37 • Open noon–4pm Tue–Sun • Adm for adults; Wed free • www.orlogsmuseet.d*

Operaen
9 The Opera House is the first major public building to be built in the Holmen area since the

navy vacated the docks in 1979. Architect Henning Larsen emphasized its location near the water with large glass windows and no pillars on the ground floor. The interior has a maritime feel as well, with balconies, open spaces and white railings. The position of the Opera House caused much controversy when it was built, especially in relation to the Amalienborg, which lies directly opposite it on the other side of the Sound. The design of the Opera House was also the cause of a little bit of friction when its benefactor, industrialist Mærsk McKinney Møller, insisted that his own architectural ideas also be incorporated into the construction *(see p8)*.

10 Gammel Dok

Gammel Dok (which means "Old Dock") was built in 1739, a time when the navy's ships moored alongside. The warehouse dates back to 1882 and now houses the Danish Architecture Centre. It holds exhibitions and provides a working space for young artists and architects who win scholarships to study here. A café on the first floor offers great views over the water. ◈ *Map L5 • Dansk Arkitektur Centre, Strandgade 27B • 32 57 19 30 • Open 10am–5pm (to 9pm Wed) • Adm for adults; free 5–9pm • www.dac.dk*

Harbour Tour

Walking Tour

Morning

🕐 Start at the Knippelsbro Bridge by the **Børsen** *(see p36)*. Built in 1937, the bridge takes its name from Hans Knip, the tollkeeper of the first bridge built here in the 17th century. Turn right to visit **Christians Kirke** on Strandgade *(see p89)*. Then, retrace your steps and cross Torvegade, walking right up to the corner of Sankt Annæ Gade. At the corner is No 32 (built in 1622–24), said to be the oldest house in Christianshavn. Turn right and then left on to **Overgaden Oven Vandet** and walk along the canal. Pop inside the **Royal Danish Naval Museum** for a quick visit. If you are curious about **Christiania** *(see p89)*, take a right down Brobergsgade, cross Prinsessegade and pass through the gate reading "you are now leaving the EU". If you are not going to the opera in the evening, continue along the canal-side and take a right turn at Bodenhoffs Plads, then a left onto Værftsbroen. Keep walking (or take the bus 66) towards the **Opera House**. Hop on a Harbour bus back to Knippelsbro for lunch at **Café Wilder** *(see p93)* and head down Sankt Annæ Gade to visit **Vor Frelsers Kirke** *(see p89)*.

Afternoon

Spend the afternoon shopping. If you are in the mood for a drink, there are cafés along the Christianshavns Kanal. Linger over supper at **L'Altro** on Torvegade *(see p92)* or catch a performance at the **Opera House** *(see p8)* (taking the bus 66 or the water bus from Knippelsbro).

Left **Mo Christianshavn** Right **Inblik**

TOP 10 Shopping

1 Mo Christianshavn
This shop, with a workshop on the premises, is owned by Mo, a jewellery designer. ❧ *Map L5 • Torvegade 24 • 32 12 02 09 • www.mo.dk*

2 Bit Antik
This tiny shop is filled with pieces from Denmark's yester-years. Among the antiques and knick-knacks are old dolls and doll houses, books, glasses, sculpture and porcelain. ❧ *Map L6 • Prinsessegade 17B • 32 54 09 62 • www.bitantik.dk*

3 Porte à Gauche
This trendy boutique offers Scandinavian designer wear for women. You will also find classic, exotic Julie Sandlau jewellery. ❧ *Map L5 • Torvegade 20 • 32 54 01 40 • www.porteagauche.dk*

4 Aurum
Original jewellery designs are produced by Marco and Carolina Vallejo at Aurum. Many materials, including precious stones, are used to create these unique pieces. ❧ *Map L6 • Wildersgade 26 • 32 96 34 22*

5 Inblik
This delightful gift shop has an eclectic collection, including stylish lighters and gadgets, shoes and jewellery, children's games and unusual photo frames. ❧ *Map L5 • Torvegade 38 • 32 57 65 61*

6 Lagkagehuset Bakery
Well known for its breads, cakes and pastries, this bakery has a fine selection of goodies during Christmas. ❧ *Map L6 • Torvegade 45 • 32 57 36 07 • Open Su.*

7 Pang Christianshavn
This shop sells gifts, clothes and shoes, as well as all kinds of kitschy items for the home in bright colours. ❧ *Map L6 • Dronningensgade 46 • 32 96 68 80 • www.pangchristianshavn.dk*

8 Hilbert København
Jewellery at this shop, run by goldsmith Morten Hilbert, is made to order. ❧ *Map L6 • Sankt Annæ Gade 24 • 33 93 53 01*

9 Cibi e Vini
This Italian delicatessen sells organic wine, fresh bread, pasta, pesto and meats. ❧ *Map L5 • Torvegade 28 • 32 57 77 98 • www.cibievini.dk*

10 Yo-Yo
Owned by former super-model Helena Christensen's mother, it sells clothes and accessories the family no longer needs. ❧ *Map L6 • Sankt Annæ Gade 3 • 20 46 31 81*

Price Categories

For a three-course meal for one without alcohol, including taxes and extra charges.

⑩	up to Dkr200
⑩⑩	200–250
⑩⑩⑩	250–350
⑩⑩⑩⑩	350–450
⑩⑩⑩⑩⑩	over Dkr450

Sofiekælderen

🔟 Cafés, Bars and Restaurants

1 Era Ora
One of the best Italian restaurants in Denmark, Era Ora offers warm service in a tranquil setting. There is a changing set menu with delicious courses and a vast wine list. For a cheaper meal, try the lunch menu. ◈ Map L6 • Overgaden Neden Vandet 33B • 32 54 06 93 • Closed Sun • Book ahead • www.era-ora.dk • ⑩⑩⑩⑩⑩

2 L'Altro
Relish homely Umbrian-Tuscan dishes in the relaxed atmosphere of this antiristorante, 1950s Italian expression that means "to dine at home". ◈ Map L6 • Torvegade 62 • 32 54 54 06 • Closed Sun • www.laltro.dk • ⑩⑩⑩⑩

3 Spicy Kitchen Cafe
This cosy Indian-Pakistani restaurant is a big hit with the locals. ◈ Map L6 • Torvegade 56 • 32 95 28 29 • ⑩

4 Luna's Diner
Popular American-style diner in the heart of Christianshavn. Known for its burgers, breakfast specials, and vegetarian options. ◈ Map L6 • Sankt Annæ Gade 5 • 32 54 20 00 • www.cafeluna.dk • ⑩

5 Sofiekælderen
This café-bar is so close to the water, you could climb down to the boats moored alongside. Enjoy a night out at its famous bar and night-club. ◈ Map L6 • Overgaden Oven Vandet 32 • 32 57 77 01 • www.sofiakaelderen.dk • ⑩

6 Café Wilder
Enjoy good French-Italian-inspired food and coffee at this café. ◈ Map L5 • Wildersgade 56 • 32 54 71 83 • www.cafewilder.dk • ⑩

7 Noma
This award-winning restaurant serves excellent gourmet cuisine, made with fresh seasonal Scandinavian produce. ◈ Map M5 • Strandgade 93 • 32 96 32 97 • Book ahead • www.noma.dk • ⑩⑩⑩⑩⑩

8 Rabes Have
Opened for local soldiers and sailors in 1632, this is the oldest pub in Copenhagen. ◈ Map K6 • Langebrogade 8 • 32 57 34 17 • Open until 5pm only • Closed Mon–Tue • ⑩

9 Bastionen & Løven
Famous for its large brunch, but also a pretty spot for a romantic evening. ◈ Map L6 • Christianshavns Voldgade 50 • 32 95 09 40 • ⑩⑩⑩⑩

🔟 Oven Vande Café
Enjoy tasty salads, soups and paninis at this café. ◈ Map L5 • Overgaden Oven Vandet 44 • 32 95 96 02 • www.cafeovenvande.dk • ⑩⑩

Left **Ordrupgaard** Right **Helsingør**

Beyond Copenhagen

ALTHOUGH COPENHAGEN ITSELF *will easily keep you entertained for several days, the area around the city offers many opportunities for days out. Roskilde and Helsingør provide a taste of Nordic history, right from the Viking era to the founding of Copenhagen. Get a sense of medieval maritime defense of the Sound at Helsingør's Kronborg Slot and explore the royal lifestyle in the 17th and 18th centuries at Frederiksborg and Charlottenlund. Art and literature lovers can drop in at Arken, Louisiana, Ordrupgaard and the Karen Blixen Museum, home to internationally acclaimed collections. Brede Værk and the Akvarium are a must-visit for kids.*

Frederiksborg Slot

Charlottenlund Slotshave

🔟 Sights

1. Roskilde
2. Louisiana Museum
3. Brede Værk
4. Helsingør
5. Arken Museum for Moderne Kunst
6. Karen Blixen Museum
7. Ordrupgaard
8. Frederiksborg Slot
9. Charlottenlund Slotshave
10. Akvarium

Preceding pages: **Interior of Den Sorte Diamant.**

1 Roskilde

Roskilde, a mere 25 minutes away from the city centre by train, makes for a fascinating day out. Older than Copenhagen itself, this was the original seat for Absalon, Bishop of Roskilde and founder of the city. Here you will find a medieval cathedral, a royal burial site and the wonderful Viking Ship Museum, which holds shipwrights' workshops (see p100).

2 Louisiana Museum

This should be high on the list for modern art enthusiasts. The museum houses an impressive selection of works by international artists like Picasso, Alberto Giacometti and Francis Bacon, and Danish masters like Asger Jorn and Per Kirkeby. There is also a children's wing here, which offers art-related activities for kids between 3 and 16 years (call for details). The seaside location, extensive sculpture park and excellent café make the museum even more appealing (see also p101). ◉ Map E1 • Gammel Strandvej 13, Humlebæk • 49 10 07 19 • Open 11am–10pm Tue–Fri, 11am–6pm Sat–Sun • Adm for adults; free for under-18s, free with Copenhagen Card • Guided tours available in English; book ahead • Dis access • www.louisiana.dk

Café in Louisiana Museum

Roskilde

3 Brede Værk

An annex to the Nationalmuseet (see pp26–7), this former textile mill has been transformed into a vast, permanent, interactive exhibition, detailing Denmark's industrial revolution. Exhibits offer visitors a glimpse into the life of an ordinary textile worker, and include a tiny, furnished flat from the 1950s. In the engine room the whole family can work together to shovel coal to create energy, produce goods on the assembly line and finally try to manage the sale of clothing. ◉ Map B2 • I.C. Modewegsvej, Kongens Lyngby • 33 47 38 00 • Open Apr–Oct 10am–5pm Tue–Sun • Free • www.bredevaerk.natmus.dk

4 Helsingør

In the 1400s, this harbour town levied tax on all sea traffic that passed through the Sound, which is just 4 km (2.5 miles) wide at this point – the town name translates as "Penny Sound". Apart from a pretty medieval centre, other sights include the 16th-century castle, Kronborg Slot, the Carmelite monastery and the Teknisk Museum of planes, trains and automobiles (see p102).

Around Town – Beyond Copenhagen

5 Arken Museum for Moderne Kunst

This wonderful museum houses a rotating permanent collection of contemporary international and Danish art, along with temporary exhibitions. The white, ship-like museum building, designed by Danish architect Søren Lund, is like an exhibit in itself. It offers great views of the sand dunes and the sea at Køge Bugt. ◎ *Map B3 • Skovvej 100, Ishøj • 43 54 02 22; Special tours: 43 57 34 55 • Open 10am–5pm Tue, Thu–Sun; 10am–9pm Wed • Adm; free for under-18s; free with Copenhagen Card • www.arken.dk*

6 Karen Blixen Museum

Karen Blixen (pen name: Isak Dinesen), author of the novel *Out of Africa,* was born here in 1885. Blixen returned in 1931 after the death of her lover, Denys Finch Hatton. The house is exactly as it was when she lived here. You can see the furniture she brought back from Nairobi, including Hatton's favourite chair. The museum holds exhibitions of her paintings and drawings, letters, a slide show of her life in Africa, readings by Blixen herself and a garden. You can also visit her grave at the foot of Ewald's Hill. ◎ *Map B2 • Rungsted Strandvej 111, Rungsted Kyst • 45 57 10 57*

• *Open May–Sep 10am–5pm Tue-Sun; Oct-Apr 1–4pm Wed–Fri, 11am–4pm Sat–Sun* • *Adm; free for under-14s; free with Copenhagen Card • Book ahead for guided tours in foreign languages • www.karen-blixen.dk*

7 Ordrupgaard

This art gallery houses a superb collection of French Impressionist art and works by 19th- and 20th-century Danish artists. The building is a 19th-century mansion with a modern extension by architect Zaha Hadid ◎ *Map B2 • Vilvordevej 110, Charlottenlund • 39 64 11 83 • Open 1–5pm Tue, Thu–Fri, 10am–6pm Wed, 11am–5pm Sat–Sun* • *Adm; free for under-18s; free with Copenhagen Card • Free audio guide* • *Book ahead for guided tours in foreign languages • www.ordrupgaard.dk*

8 Frederiksborg Slot

Built in 1560 by the architect king, Christian IV, this copper-turreted, fairy-tale castle stands next to a lake and is surrounded by elaborately-designed Baroque gardens. The interior is a mix of Renaissance and Rococo decor. After a fire in 1859, the castle was rescued from ruin by JC Jacobsen (of Carlsberg fame), who founded a national history museum here. Be sure to visit the beautiful chapel. ◎ *Map B1*

Karen Blixen Museum

Danmarks Akvarium

- DK-3400 Hillerød • 48 26 04 39
- Open Apr–Oct 10am–5pm; Nov–Mar 11am–3pm • Baroque Gardens: Oct–Mar 8am–6pm daily; Apr–Sep 8am–9pm daily
- Adm; free with Copenhagen Card
- www.frederiksborgmuseet.dk

Charlottenlund Slotshave

The park around Charlottenlund Palace is a 16-minute train ride from the city centre. Redesigned in the Romantic English style in the 19th century, the park's attractions include a charming thatched cottage, once lodgings for the Royal Life Guards. The French Renaissance chateau-style palace is closed to the public. ◎ Map B2 • www.ses.dk

Danmarks Akvarium

Over 285 marine species from the world over are housed in over 70 aquariums at this museum. Everything from piranhas to turtles of all sizes (some the size of your little finger) are found here. One of the "residents" is said to have swum to the North Sea coast all the way from the Mediterranean Sea. ◎ Map B2
- Kavalergården 1, Charlottenlund
- 39 62 32 83 • Open Feb–May & Sep–Oct 10am–5pm; Jun–Aug 10am–6pm; Nov–Jan 10am–4pm; also to 8pm Wed all year • Adm • www.akvarium.dk

Day Tour

Morning

Start your day by hopping onto a train at Hovedbanegården and heading to **Helsingør**. Visit **Kronborg Slot** in Helsingør before lunch, and then wander around the old town (see pp97 and 102). Alternatively, get off the train at **Humlebæk** and visit the **Louisiana Museum** (see p97). If at Helsingør, have an open sandwich and a beer at one of the many pubs at the town square; if in Louisiana, have lunch at the garden café.

Afternoon

After lunch, if you are in Helsingør, wander through the medieval streets, especially **Strandgade** and **Stengade** (see p102). Visit the medieval **Domkirke**, the **Teknisk Museum** and the **Bymuseum** (see p102), housed in a Carmelite monastery dating back to 1516. If in Louisiana, return to the station and take a train to Rungsted Kyst and drop in at the **Karen Blixen Museum**; try one of the home-made cakes at the café. Or get off the train at Klampenborg to see the fascinating Impressionist paintings at **Ordrupgaard**. If you are in Helsingør or the **Karen Blixen Museum**, start heading back towards Copenhagen in the early evening, stopping at Klampenborg for an evening of entertainment at the **Bakken Fun Fair**. You can also catch a bite to eat here. If you are at Ordrupgaard, visit the café and then walk to the fun fair; either cut through the park or use the main road. On weekdays, you can wander around the Louisiana Museum till 10pm.

Left **Vikingeskibsmuseet** Centre **Roskilde Kloster** Right **Hestetorvet**

TOP 10 Roskilde

1 Roskilde Domkirke
This magnificent cathedral holds the remains of 39 Danish monarchs. ◎ *Map P6 • Domkirke-stræde 10 • 46 35 16 24 • Open Apr–Sep 9am–5pm Mon–Sat, 12:30–5pm Sun; Oct–Mar 10am–4pm Tue–Sat, 12:30–4pm Sun • Adm; free for under-7s and with Copenhagen Card • www.roskildedomkirke.dk*

2 Stændertorvet
This small square in front of the Town Hall has been a market place since the Middle Ages. ◎ *Map P6 • Markets on Wed & Sat*

3 Roskilde Palace
Built in 1733–36 for royal visitors, this yellow, four-wing Baroque building houses the Museum of Contemporary Art and the Palace Wing. ◎ *Map P6 • Stændertorvet 3 • Museum: 46 31 65 70; Open 11am–5pm Tue–Fri, noon–4pm Sat & Sun • Palace Wing 46 32 14 70; Open mid-May–mid-Sep 11am–4pm daily • Adm for adults • www. samtidskunst.dk*

4 Roskilde Museum
This museum illustrates Roskilde's history from the time when it was Denmark's first capital. ◎ *Map P5 • Sankt Ols Gade 15–18 • 46 31 65 00 • Open 11am–4pm daily, closed 24, 25, 31 Dec & 1 Jan • Adm for adults; free with Copenhagen Card • www.roskildemuseum.dk*

5 Roskilde Kloster
This manor was bought in 1699 by two aristocratic women who converted it into a home for unmarried mothers. ◎ *Map P6 • Sankt Pederstraede 8 • 46 35 02 19 • www.roskildekloster.dk*

6 Kirkegård
Now a park, this medieval churchyard holds the graves of many prominent Roskilde citizens. ◎ *Map Q6*

7 Hestetorvet
The Horse Market is set in what was Roskilde's largest square for centuries. Look out for the three giant vases that commemorate Roskilde's millennium in 1998. ◎ *Map Q6*

8 Vikingeskibsmuseet
The popular Viking Ship Museum displays five 1,000-year-old Viking vessels that were re-covered from the watery depths in 1962: a warship, longship, ferry and deep sea vessel. Viking-ship boat trips are available in the summer *(see below)*. ◎ *Map P4 • Vindeboder 12 • 46 30 02 00 • Open 10am–5pm daily • Adm for adults; free for under-18s • www.vikingeskibsmuseet.dk*

9 Viking Ship Trips
Sail for 50 minutes in a replica of a 1,000-year-old Viking warship. ◎ *Map P4 • Vikingeskibs-museet, Vindeboder 12 • 46 30 02 53 • www.vikingeskibsmuseet.dk*

10 Skomagergade & Algade
The city's two main, beauti-fully paved streets, are lined with shops and cafés. ◎ *Map P6*

Roskilde is home to one of the largest open-air music festivals in Europe, usually the first week in July (www.roskilde-festival.dk).

Left **Eyes (1997) in the sculpture park** Right **Two Piece Reclining Figure No. 5 1963–64**

TOP 10 Louisiana Museum

1 Big Thumb 1968
This striking, 2-m (6-ft) tall bronze thumb is modelled after the thumb of its creator, French sculptor César Baldaccini (1921–98).

2 Dead Drunk Danes 1960
Rebel artist Asger Jorn (1914–1973) was awarded the Guggenheim International Award for this expressive abstract painting. However, he rejected the accolade and sent Harry Guggenheim an infuriated telegram: "Go to hell with your money bastard *stop* Never asked for it *stop* Against all decency to mix artist against his will in your publicity *stop*".

3 Spider Couple 2003
Louise Bourgeois' gigantic sculpture depicts a smaller spider seeking refuge within the limbs of a larger one. Spiders are a recurring motif in this artist's work.

4 Close Cover Before Striking 1962
An early Warhol acrylic painting in the pop art style. Here, the image of a matchbook is enlarged to the point of abstraction.

5 Déjeuner sur l'Herbe (1961)
Painted by Pablo Picasso (1881–1973), this abstract work pays homage to Edouard Manet's revolutionary painting of 1862–63, in which a nude woman sits in a classical setting, having a picnic with two clothed modern men.

6 Alberto Giacometti Collection
The museum owns an impressive collection of 13 sculptures and several drawings by Alberto Giacometti (1901–66). The elongated figures with rough textures are reminiscent of African sculpture.

7 Two Piece Reclining Figure No. 5 1963–64
This bronze work by Henry Moore (1898–1986) occupies a beautiful spot between the trees, its humanoid, organic forms melding with the landscape.

8 Homage to the Yellow Square: Climate 1962
This is part of the series titled *Homage to the Square* by Josef Albers (1888–1976), the influential Bauhaus artist who explored the chromatic relationship of different coloured flat squares.

9 Figures in a Landscape (1977)
In this painting by Roy Lichtenstein (1923–97), an exponent of Pop Art, symbols and images are broken down in a Cubist style and set in a surreal landscape.

10 The Sculpture Park
In the museum's sculpture park, the visual arts, architecture and landscapes exist in unity; the sculptures create silhouettes against the sky, and the gardens enhance the sculptures' appeal. The views are as much a part of the park's charm as its exhibits.

Left **Marienlyst Slot** Right **Axeltorv**

Helsingør

Kronborg Slot
Famous as the setting of Shakespeare's play *Hamlet*, this castle was first built in 1420. Its Great Hall is the largest in Europe. ◈ *Map Q2 • Kronborg 2C • 49 21 30 78 • Open May–Sep 10:30am–5pm daily; Oct 11am–4pm Tue–Sun; Nov–Mar 11am–3pm Tue–Sun • Adm • www.kronborg.dk*

Danmarks Teknisk Museum
The collection of machines here, include steam engines, cars (one dating back to 1887) and aeroplanes. ◈ *Fabriksvej 25 • 49 22 26 11 • Open 10am–5pm Tue–Sun; Mon in July & school holidays • Adm; free with Copenhagen Card • www.tekniskmuseum.dk*

Festivals
Helsingør's summer festivals include the Maritime Festival Baltic Sail, Sunset Jazz Festival in Hornbæk, and the Hamlet Festival every August at Kronborg. ◈ *www.visithelsingor.dk*

Karmeliterklosteret
This 15th century Gothic-style monastery belonged to the Carmelite Order. ◈ *Map P2 • Sankt Anna Gade 38 • 49 21 17 74 • Church open: mid-May–mid-Sep 10am–3pm daily; mid-Sep–mid-May 10am–2pm daily • Tours of monastery must be booked • Adm (church free) • www.sctmariae.dk*

Helsingør Bymuseum
Next door to the Carmelite Monastery, the Town Museum was originally used as a hospital for sailors. A permanent exhibition recalls the hospital's history and other details about this medieval town. ◈ *Map P2 • Sankt Anna Gade 36 • 49 28 18 00 • noon– 4pm daily • www. helsingor.dk/museum*

Axeltorv
This main square features a statue of Erik of Pomerania, the Polish prince who ruled Denmark from 1397–1439. ◈ *Map P2*

Stengade & Strandgade
Stengade is a pedestrianized street in the medieval quarter. Some houses on Strandgade date back to the 1400s. ◈ *Map P3*

Sankt Olai Kirke (Helsingør Domkirke)
Note the 15th-century crucifix, the 1568 Renaissance pulpit, the 1575 baptismal font and the carved wooden altar. ◈ *Map P2 • Sankt Anna Gade 12 • 49 21 04 43 • Open May–Aug 10am–4pm Mon–Fri; Sep–Apr 10am–2pm Mon–Fri • www.helsingordomkirke.dk*

Marienlyst Slot
Named after Frederik V's wife Juliana Maria, this Neo-Classical manor is now a museum. Its 18th-century interiors are well preserved. ◈ *Map N1 • Marienlyst Allé 32 • 49 28 18 30 • Closed for renovation • Adm for adults; free with Copenhagen Card*

Øresundakvariet
This aquarium has a variety of tropical fish and Baltic species. ◈ *Map P1 • Strandpromenaden 5 • 35 32 19 70 • Open Jun–Aug 10am–5pm daily; Sep–May 10am–4pm Mon–Fri, 10am–5pm Sat–Sun • Adm; free with Copenhagen Card*

Around Town – Beyond Copenhagen

For information on the season of Shakespeare's plays performed each August at Kronborg Castle, visit www.hamletsommer.dk.

Price Categories

For a three-course meal for one without alcohol, including taxes and extra charges.

⊗	up to Dkr200
⊗⊗	200–250
⊗⊗⊗	250–350
⊗⊗⊗⊗	350–450
⊗⊗⊗⊗⊗	over Dkr450

Søstrene Olsen

Places To Eat

1 Café Bomhuset
An upscale alternative to the typical outdoor café with food to match. The large terrace is popular. ⊗ *Map B2 • Skovridderkroen, Strandvejen 235, Charlottenlund • 39 65 67 00 • 11am–9pm daily (Sat–Sun from 10am) • www.cafebomhuset.dk • ⊗⊗⊗*

2 Restaurant Sletten
Sharing its owners with Formel B *(see p48)*, Sletten serves French cuisine at lower prices, with the bonus of a sea view. ⊗ *Map B2 • Gl.Strandvej 137, Humlebæk • 49 19 13 21 • wwwsletten.dk • ⊗⊗⊗⊗*

3 Restaurant Jacobsen
Dine in style on the famous Arne Jacobsen chairs, and even use Jacobsen cutlery. The menu spans modern Italian, French and Danish cuisine. Fish is especially good. ⊗ *Map B2 • Strandvejen 449, Klampenborg • 39 63 43 22 • Closed Mon • www.restaurantjacobsen.dk • ⊗⊗⊗*

4 Den Gule Cottage
This timber-framed restaurant was created in 1844 by architect Bindesbøll. Dishes are prepared with fresh, seasonal ingredients. ⊗ *Map B2 • Strandvejen 506, Klampenborg • 39 64 06 91 • Closed Jan–Feb Sun; Oct–Dec & Mar Sun–Mon • www.dengulecottage.dk • ⊗⊗⊗⊗⊗*

5 Mikkelgaard
This restaurant, set on a farm with lawns down to the sea, serves good Danish food. ⊗ *Map B2 • Rungsted Strandvej 302, Hørsholm • 45 76 63 13 • Closed Mon; Oct–Apr Sun–Tue • Lunch only Sun • www.mikkelgaard.dk • ⊗⊗⊗⊗*

6 Restaurant Gilleleje Havn
Enjoy traditional Danish seafood at this fine old seamen's inn (1895) on the harbour. After the meal, stroll along the beautiful sandy beach. ⊗ *Map A1 • Havnevej 14, Gilleleje • 48 30 30 39 • Closed Mon–Wed • www.gillelejehavn.dk • ⊗⊗⊗*

7 Nokken
This smart, seaside restaurant serves modern Mediterranean dishes with a Danish twist. ⊗ *Map B2 • Rungsted Havn 44, Rungsted • 45 57 13 14 • www.nokken.dk • ⊗⊗⊗⊗*

8 Røgeriet Rungsted
Try the popular smoked fish served at this old smokery. ⊗ *Map B2 • Rungsted Havn 22, Rungsted • 45 76 06 08 • ⊗⊗⊗⊗⊗*

9 Restaurant Køllesgaard
Køllesgaard serves a café-style lunch and an upmarket Danish-French evening menu. Enjoy sea views and outdoor seating in summer. ⊗ *Map B2 • Ny Strandvej 21, Humlebæk • 49 19 15 05 • www.restaurantkoellesgaard.dk • ⊗⊗⊗⊗*

10 Søstrene Olsen
The food at this cottage-style restaurant is delicious. The seafood is particularly good. ⊗ *Map B1 • Øresundsvej 10, Hornbæk • 49 70 05 50 • Closed Tue–Wed • www.sostreneolsen.dk • ⊗⊗⊗⊗*

Around Town – Beyond Copenhagen

STREETSMART

COPENHAGEN'S TOP 10

Left **An SAS plane** Right **International ferry**

TOP 10 Getting There and Around

1 Arriving By Air
Airlines that serve Copenhagen directly are Scandinavian Airlines (SAS), Aer Lingus, British Airways, easyJet, Cimber Sterling and Norwegian. The airport is 12 km (7 miles) away from the city; it takes about 15 mins to get to the city by train or Metro, or 45 mins by bus (both cost the same). You will also find a taxi rank just outside the airport (terminal 3).

2 Arriving By Train
International trains run to and from many European cities, including Hamburg and Berlin. All international trains stop at Hovedbanegården, the city's main station.

3 Arriving By Road
If driving into Copenhagen from Sweden, you can take the Øresund bridge from Malmø. If driving in from Germany and crossing the island of Funen, you can take the Great Belt Bridge to Sjælland, the island on which the city is built. Both bridges exact a toll.

4 Arriving By Ferry
You can take a Polferries ferry from Poland (Swinoujscie) or a DFDS Seaways ferry from Norway (Oslo). Ferries from the UK (Harwich) stop at Esbjerg; from here, you can take a train to Copenhagen or drive 300 km (186 miles) on the E20 motorway.

5 Local Public Transport
The bus, local (S) train and Metro systems are frequent and efficient. In Greater Copenhagen, you can use a single ticket or discount clip card to transfer between these three systems. These cards are available for 10 journeys and work out cheaper than the basic tickets available. www.dsb.dk/english

6 Harbour Buses
Harbour buses (901 and 902) run the length of the harbour between Den Sorte Diamant and Gefionspringvandet. Daily 6am–6pm/7pm, every 10 mins.

7 Taxis & Rickshaws
Taxis have a FRI (free) sign on the roof. You can pay by credit card and also get receipts. Catch the cycle rickshaws for short rides at Storkespringvandet, Tivoli, Rådhuspladsen and Nyhavn.

8 Driving & Parking
You can drive if you are over 18 and hold a valid licence. Always carry the registration papers and reflecting triangle. *Parkering forbudt* means no parking within certain time limits. Motoring offences attract on-the-spot fines.

9 Bicycles
Bicycles offer a great way to enjoy more of Copenhagen in a short period of time. There are cycle paths throughout the city. Free city bikes are available from mid-April to mid-December at 110 special stands around the city.

10 On Foot
Copenhagen is a lovely place to walk around. As it is relatively small, many of the sites are a short walk away from each other, unless you plan on heading out to Nørrebro or crossing town. Tourist signposting is helpful.

Left **Airport information board** Centre **Tourist information sign** Right **Copenhagen Right Now**

10 General Information

Best Time to Visit
1 Summertime is ideal since you can enjoy as many as 16–18 hours of daylight on clear days. Christmas is also fun, with fairy lights and celebrations at Tivoli, the open-air ice rink at Kongens Nytorv and plenty of markets, concerts and other entertainment. There is plenty for kids to do in other Danish school holidays as well: week 7 July to mid-August, and week 42. The only time you might want to avoid, due to chilly winds and the limited hours of daylight (only seven), is Dec–Jan.

Visas
2 European Union citizens do not require a visa to enter Denmark and can stay for up to 90 days. Others should check whether their country has reciprocal agreements on waiving visa requirements. Foreign nationals who wish to work in Copenhagen must have work and residence permit for paid or unpaid work. ✆ www.nyidanmark. dk/en-us/coming_to_dk/ coming_to_dk.htm

Duty Free Goods & Customs
3 Denmark imposes a limit on what can be brought into the country. Do not carry food articles that are not vacuum-packed by the

manufacturer. Articles in commercial quantities and presents valued at more than 1,350kr are subject to customs duty. US citizens are liable to pay duty if carrying goods worth more than $400. Many shops offer tax-free shopping for non-EU visitors for a minimum purchase of 300kr; remember to collect a Global Refund Tax Free Cheque from the store, so you can apply for a 13–19 per cent refund. ✆ www. globalrefund.com

Tourist Information
4 Copenhagen's visitors' centre, called Copenhagen Right Now, is close to the main station. It offers a wealth of information, as well as hotel bookings, car rental, the Copenhagen Card (see p111) and information about tours. ✆ Map G5 • Copenhagen Right Now, Vesterbrogade 4A • 70 22 24 42 • www. visitcopenhagen.com

Opening Hours
5 Opening hours for shops are: Mon–Thu 9:30am/10am–5:30pm; Fri 9:30am/10am– 7pm/8pm; Sat 9:30am/ 10am–noon/1pm (to 5pm on the first Saturday of the month). Weekend hours may be extended in tourist areas, especially in summer. Most museums are closed on Mondays.

Weekly Listings
6 The Copenhagen Post (each Friday) provides a useful guide to events taking place in the city. Danish speakers can check the Friday guide sections of Politiken and Berlingske.

Websites
7 Tourist board web-sites provide useful information. Other websites are listed below. ✆ www. visitcopenhagen.com • www.visitdenmark.dk • www.aok.dk/section/ english • www.ctw.dk

Public Holidays
8 Public holidays include New Year's Day, Maundy Thursday, Good Friday, Easter Monday, Common Prayer's Day, Ascension Day, Whit Monday and Christmas.

Admission Prices
9 Some museums are always free, others are mostly free on Wednesdays. The Copenhagen Card offers discounts and allows entry to 65 attractions and museums.

For Children
10 Several museums have children's facilities, and most restaurants provide high chairs – some even have special children's menus (call to check). Hotels like the Admiral and DGI-Byen also offer babysitting services. The airport has play areas, baby-changing facilities and buggies.

Left **A typical pharmacy** Right **Police van**

TOP 10 Health and Security

1 Health Insurance & Precautions

Although emergency medical treatment is free, make sure you have suitable travel insurance. EU nationals should bring their European Health Insurance cards. Visitors from Schengen countries (several EU countries plus Iceland, Norway and Switzerland) can carry up to 30 days' supply of prescribed medication; others must carry no more than 14 days' supply. Documents stating the need for the medication may be required.

2 Pharmacies

Pharmacies have a green sign saying "A" (*Apotek*). Prescription medication can only be bought at pharmacies. Credit cards are not accepted; full payment is required. 🛇 *Steno Apotek, Vesterbrogade 6C (opp. main station)*

3 Medical Treatment

Tourists are covered by public health services as per the agreement between Denmark and their home country. Emergency hospital treatment is free for all tourists, unless the medical facility determines that the emergency occurred as a result of a pre-existing condition. Refunds for doctor's fees can be obtained from the nearest municipal or health insurance office before leaving Denmark.

4 Personal Safety

Copenhagen is a safe city, but visitors must take precautions. Make sure your bags are closed securely and your credit cards, mobile and money are kept in a safe place. Also, avoid carrying large amounts of cash. If you are a victim of a crime, contact the police immediately *(see below)*.

5 Police

To file reports, contact the nearest police station *(see Directory)*. In a crisis, call the emergency services number.

6 Dental Treatment

Head to Dentist Tandlægevagten (Oslo Plads 14, tel. 35 38 02 51), open 8am–9:30pm Mon–Fri, 10am–noon Sat–Sun. Be prepared to pay at least 150kr on the spot.

7 Doctors & Hospitals

Outside office hours, call Doctor On Call. If an emergency arises, go to the Accident and Emergency section of any hospital *(see Directory)*.

8 Theft

Report theft at a police station immediately *(see Directory)*; you will be issued with a crime report note, which you will need for any insurance claims.

9 Disabled Access

The tourist office, Copenhagen Right Now *(see p107)*, has a list of places that offer facilities for the disabled. You can also contact DSB Handicap *(see Directory)*.

10 Lost Property

For items lost on the bus, call 36 13 14 15; for items lost on local (S)-train: 36 14 17 01. Lost property office: 38 74 88 22.

Directory

Pharmacies
• *Steno Apotek (24 hrs): 33 14 82 66*

Police
• *Station City: Halmtorvet 20; 33 25 14 48*
• *Politivagten: Copenhagen Central Station; 33 15 38 01*
• *Slotsherrensvej (lost and found): 38 74 88 22*

Emergency Services
112

Doctors & Hospitals
• *Doctor On Call: 70 13 00 41*
• *Amager Hospital: 32 34 35 00*
• *Bispebjerg Hospital: 35 31 23 73*
• *Frederiksberg Hospital: 38 16 35 22*
• *Rigshospitalet: 33 45 35 45*

Handicap Services
• *DSB Handicap Service: 70 13 14 19*
• *4 x 35 Taxi (book ahead): 35 39 35 35*
• *Tourist office list: www.visitcopenhagen.com/composite-253.htm*

Left **Using Wi-Fi by the canal** Centre **ATM machine** Right **A Danish letterbox**

⟨10 Banking and Communications

1 Local Currency
Danish notes come in denominations of 1,000kr, 500kr, 200kr, 100kr and 50kr. Coins come in 20kr, 10kr, 5kr, 2kr, 1kr and 50 øre (half a krone).

2 Banks & ATMs
Banks are usually open Mon–Wed 10am–10pm; Thu 10am–6pm. Most ATMs are open 24 hours a day, and are usually found outside banks and Metro stations. The most popular card is Visa, but finding machines that accept MasterCard or American Express shouldn't be a problem, either.

3 Exchange
There are many exchange bureaux throughout the city. Those open for the longest include Den Danske Bank's exchange office (6am–10pm) at Copenhagen Airport, and the Forex (8am–9pm) at the Hovedbånegard station. Hotels have foreign exchange services, but the rate is lower than at banks or exchange bureaux.

4 Credit Cards
International credit cards are not always accepted, especially at small outlets. There may also be an extra charge if you pay by credit card. If you lose your credit card, call your credit card company immediately (see Directory).

5 Post Offices
Post offices are usually open Mon–Fri 9am/10am–5.30pm; Sat 9am–noon (or closed). You can arrange for a Poste Restante service at any post office. International mail arrives faster with the Faste Deliver A-mail or Prioritaire mail service.
⊛ www.postdanmark.dk

6 Telephones
The international dialling code for Denmark is +45; there are no area codes. To make international calls from Denmark, first dial 00. Public telephones accept coins and pre-paid phone cards. Insert 5–20 kr for international calls; however, you will not receive change. You cannot make collect calls to the US from public phones. For information and directory assistance, call 113.

7 Mobiles
GSM compatible mobile phones will work. There are three main service providers (see Directory). Roaming is expensive, so check your service provider's rates for calls from abroad.

8 Internet
Copenhagen's biggest Internet café is Boomtown Netcafé. Most hotels offer Internet access, many with Wi-Fi in rooms. Free Wi-Fi is also available on many buses and trains, as well as in some cafés and public spaces.

9 TV & Radio
Cable and satellite TV provide access to channels in English and other languages. Radio Denmark International (1062 Mz) broadcasts news in English at 10:30am, 5:05pm and 10pm.

10 Newspapers & Magazines
Denmark's national newspapers include: Borsen, Ekstra Bladet, Jyllands-Posten, Information and Politiken. For local news in English, get the Copenhagen Post (20kr). You can find most major UK and US newspapers in city centre kiosks.

Directory

Credit Card Companies
• AMEX: 70 20 70 97
• MasterCard: 80 01 60 98
• Visa and Other cards: 44 89 29 29
• Danish PBS 24-hr hotline (for other credit cards): 44 89 29 29
• Diners Club: 36 73 73 73

Mobile Companies
• Telenor: 72 10 01 00
• TDC-Mobil: 80 80 80 20
• Telia: 80 40 40 40

Internet Cafés
• Boomtown Netcafé: Axeltorv 1–3
• Faraos Cigarer: Skindergade 27

Left **Traffic lights at a pedestrian crossing** Right **People waiting to cross a street**

TOP 10 Things To Avoid

1 Jaywalking

The Danes hardly ever jaywalk, even if there is no traffic in either direction. If you can't resist the urge to do so, don't be surprised if a grumpy policeman decides to arrest you for breaking the law. Always cross at the pedestrian crossing when the signal turns green. For the benefit of the visually impaired, a beeping sound is emitted for the entire duration when it is safe to cross.

2 Exceeding the Speed Limit or Drinking & Driving

Exceeding the speed limit is illegal and you can be fined on the spot. If you don't pay, your car may be impounded. Drinking and driving is strictly prohibited as well. Do not drive if the level of alcohol content in your blood is more than 0.5 (two drinks). For alcohol levels of up to 1.2, a large fine is imposed. If the level is 1.2–2, you could lose your license. Levels above 2 may result in a prison sentence of two weeks or more.

3 Buying Drugs

Buying and selling drugs in Denmark is illegal, just as in most other places, and the penalties are severe. Once, buying drugs from a booth on Pusher Street in Christiania was almost *de rigueur* for young visitors. However, Pusher Street has now been shut down and drugs cannot be bought openly.

4 Forgetting to Clip Tickets on Public Transport

Always remember to clip your ticket to validate it when you travel on public transport. Clipping machines can be found on buses and on platforms of train and Metro stations. If you do not clip your ticket, you can be fined by inspectors.

5 Visiting Museums on Monday Without Checking

Most museums are shut on Mondays, though a few are closed on Tuesdays instead. So, check in advance for frustration-free sightseeing.

6 Stepping Out in Front of a Bike

Visitors who are not used to having cycle lanes in their cities might mistake this area for part of the pavement. However, bikes have right of way here. Remember to treat cycle lanes as you would the rest of the road.

7 Grumbling in English

Practically everyone below the age of 70 (and many above) speak excellent English, as they have been watching English and American films and TV for a long time. So, if you grumble in English, everyone from the bus driver up will know exactly what you are saying.

8 Praising the Swedes

The Danes and their neighbours, the Swedes, have been at loggerheads for centuries. These days, the Danes continue to be rude about the Swedes, but in a tongue-in-cheek way. However, they often do mean it when they say that the Swedes travel to Copenhagen only to buy alcohol, as it is less expensive here.

9 Insulting the Royal Family

The Danes are very respectful of their royal family, especially the present queen. Insulting them is highly inadvisable; it would be similar to (if not a little worse) insulting someone's favourite sports team. However unintentional it may be, it could damage your relations with your hosts – especially the older generation.

10 Not Making Eye Contact When "Skolling" a Drink

It is considered rude if you don't lock your gaze with your drinking partner and say a toast and say "*Skål*". This tradition of "skolling" dates back to the Vikings, who used to chop off the heads of vanquished enemy chiefs and drink out of their skulls.

Left **Café in Vesterbro** Right **Gardens of the Royal Library**

🔟 Copenhagen on a Budget

1 Reservations
Make your hotel reservations well in advance to get the best deals. The peak season is usually Apr/May–Sept/Oct. Online hotel prices are often cheaper and many hotels have lower rates at weekends, but it's a good idea to ring the hotel and ask about their best prices and deals.

2 Sights
A well-planned trip can be surprisingly inexpensive. Walking the streets is free and also fascinating. Discount clip cards (see p106) reduce your expense on public transport. Parks and gardens (except Tivoli) are free, and often host free entertainment, especially in the summer. Several state-run museums are free; others are free on Wednesdays or Sundays. The Danish National Theatre sells unsold tickets at half price after 4pm on the day of the performance. ◊ *Danish National Theatre box office: Tordenskjoldsgade 7*

3 The Copenhagen Card
The Copenhagen Card is a good investment, offering lots of great discounts for sightseeing and transport. For information, or to buy the Copenhagen Card in advance (minimum of 10 days), visit the Copenhagen Visitors' Centre website (see p107).

4 Cheap Eats
As in most other places, pizza and pasta dishes are cheap in Copenhagen. Fast food outlets are plentiful, and you can get a sandwich or a burger and chips for under 50kr. If you want something more substantial for under 150kr, a main course, bread and a glass of wine or beer in a café will easily fit your budget. Some restaurants, especially Thai, offer reasonably priced buffet lunches.

5 Hotel Breakfasts
Although breakfast is a modest affair for most Danes, visitors are spoiled for choice at hotels. Eat-all-you-want breakfasts offer good value for money, even at 100–150kr – especially if you can fill up for the day. Some hotels include breakfast in the price of the room, so check when you book.

6 Meals
Lunch (*Frokost*) is served from noon–2pm. Dinner (*Aftensmad*) is usually served from 6pm–9:30pm/10pm, although you can call to check if the kitchen is open after that. Dinner often costs more, but you are served larger portions. Late night snacks are limited to hot dogs or kebabs from a stall.

7 Tipping
Tips are usually included in bills at restaurants and hotels, so it is not considered rude if you don't leave one. In cheaper places, rounding the bill up is perfectly acceptable. In more expensive restaurants, it is customary to leave a tip, but it can be as little as 5 per cent of the bill. You don't have to tip taxi drivers.

8 Free Music Events
Every Wednesday in the spring and summer, students from the Royal Danish Academy of Music perform classical concerts at the Theatre Museum. Look out for the street bands at the jazz festival in July (see p43) and for Friday Rock at Tivoli (see p11). ◊ www.onsdagskoncerter. dk • www.jazzfestival.dk

9 Other Free Events
During Christmas, special markets are held with some shops like the Royal Copenhagen (see p68), putting up exhibitions. Free skating is on offer at rinks at Kongens Nytorv, Frederiksberg Runddel and Blågårds Plads. Museums conduct free workshops for kids (closed 24–25 Dec).

10 Movies
Some cinemas offer lower rates from Mon–Thu before 6pm (ring to check). Between Jul–Aug, free open-air screenings are held by Zulu Sommerbio. ◊ www. zulu.dk

Left **Hotel Alexandra** Right **Palace Hotel**

🔟 Luxury Hotels

1 Palace Hotel
This Victorian hotel is part of the Scandic chain. Overlooking Rådhuspladsen, it combines traditional English decor with a modern twist. The hotel bar is popular with the locals. 🔍 *Map H5 • Rådhuspladsen 57 • 33 48 04 00 • www. palacehotel.dk • ⑩⑩⑩⑩*

2 Hotel d'Angleterre
Olden day grandeur meets modern luxury at this 250-year-old hotel. It has a plush palm court, banquet rooms, a spa and an elegant restaurant serving international cuisine. 🔍 *Map K4 • Kongens Nytorv 34 • 33 12 00 95 • www. dangleterre.dk • ⑩⑩⑩⑩⑩*

3 Hotel Alexandra
More than a century old, this excellent 3-star hotel became popular in the 1990s for its original, 20th-century furniture design, with classics ranging from Kaare Klint chairs to Akademi chandeliers designed by Poul Henningsen. There are three non-smoking floors and an allergy-tested room. 🔍 *Map G5 • HC Andersens Boulevard 8 • 33 74 44 44 • www. hotelalexandra.dk • ⑩⑩⑩⑩*

4 Hotel Front
This modern, child-friendly boutique hotel offers rooms of various sizes. Each room has been individually decorated and enhanced with attractive artwork. 🔍 *Map L4 • Skt Annæ Plads 21 • 33 13 34 00 • www. scandichotels.dk/front • ⑩⑩⑩⑩*

5 Sankt Petri
Every room of this 5-star hotel is delightfully decorated with orchids and abstract art and the bathrooms are luxurious. It has a lively glass-roofed atrium featuring international DJs, as well as a popular cocktail bar. 🔍 *Map H4 • Krystalgade 22 • 33 45 91 00 • www.hotelsktpetri. com • ⑩⑩⑩⑩⑩*

6 Kong Arthur
Close to Rosenborg Slot *(see pp20–21)*, this 4-star hotel is located inside a large courtyard. It exudes old-world charm, and offers large family rooms and a conservatory-style breakfast room. 🔍 *Map H4 • Nørre Søgade 11 • 33 11 12 12 • www. kongarthur.dk • ⑩⑩⑩⑩*

7 Nyhavn 71
This charming 4-star hotel at the end of Nyhavn was once a warehouse built to store goods from ships on the harbour. The area is very peaceful and does not suffer from noisy tourists; few wander this far down the quayside. The restaurant offers a substantial breakfast. 🔍 *Map L4 • Nyhavn 71 • 33 43 62 00 • www. 71nyhavnhotel.com • ⑩⑩⑩⑩*

8 Phoenix
Owned by the Arp-Hansen group, this comfortable 4-star hotel, just off Kongens Nytorv, is decorated in a French, Louis XIV style with contemporary colour and touch. Housed in a 17th-century building that originally belonged to an aristocratic family called Von Plessen, the hotel has a restaurant and "English pub"-style bar. 🔍 *Map L3 • Bredgade 37 • 33 95 95 00 • www. phoenixcopenhagen.dk • ⑩⑩⑩*

9 Hilton Copen-hagen Airport
This is a swanky 5-star hotel, equipped with a spa, pool, gym, three restaurants and bars and good business facilities. The decor is distinctly Scandinavian with plenty of light wood. 🔍 *Ellehammersvej, 20 Kastrup • 32 50 15 01 • www.hilton.dk • ⑩⑩⑩⑩⑩*

10 Grand Hotel
A short walk down Vesterbrogade, this classic 4-star hotel is located close to Tivoli. In the summer, you can sit in its pavement café for a spot of people-watching. The rooms are spacious and the decor traditional without being ornate. The hotel's Restaurant Frascati is very good and serves Italian cuisine. 🔍 *Map G5 • Vesterbrogade 9 • 33 27 69 00 • www. grandhotel.dk • ⑩⑩⑩*

Streetsmart

The Square

Price Categories

For a standard, double room per night (with breakfast if included), taxes and extra charges.

⑧	up to Dkr750
⑧⑧	750–1,000
⑧⑧⑧	1,000–1,300
⑧⑧⑧⑧	1,300–1,800
⑧⑧⑧⑧⑧	over Dkr1,800

⑩ Expensive Hotels

1 Hotel Twentyseven
This boutique hotel, with its minimalist decor, is centrally located not far from Strøget and Rådhuspladsen. The bars include a wine bar, cocktail lounge and the Icebar Copenhagen. ⑨ *Map H5 • Løngangstræde 27 • 70 27 56 27 • www.hotel27. dk • ⑧⑧⑧*

2 Copenhagen Plaza
Built in 1913, this hotel has been bought by Profil Hotels. It has spacious rooms and tra-ditional decor. The Library Bar, full of 18th-century books, is one of the best bars in the city. ⑨ *Map G5 • Bernstorffsgade 4 • 33 14 92 62 • www.copenhagen-plaza.hotel-rez.com • ⑧⑧⑧*

3 Imperial Hotel
Stylish and welcom-ing, this 4-star hotel has been decorated in modern Danish design and has an entire floor dedicated to the work of the Danish designer Børge Mogensen. ⑨ *Map G5 • Vester Farmimagsgade 9 • 33 12 80 00 • www. imperialhotel.dk • ⑧⑧⑧*

4 Opera
This 3-star Arp-Hansen hotel is located under the arches of the Royal theatre in a building that dates back to 1869. It has operated as a hotel since the 1950s. The decor is modern with traditional English overtones, such as Regency-striped armchairs. ⑨ *Map K4 • Tordenskjoldsgade 15 • 33 47 83 00 • www. hotelopera.dk • ⑧⑧⑧*

5 The Square
This modern 3-star hotel is located on the Town Hall square. It comes with stylish pony-hair chairs at the entrance and Arne Jacobsen chairs in the reception area. The rooms are comfortable and the breakfast on offer is excellent. ⑨ *Map H5 • Rådhuspladsen 14 • 33 38 12 00 • www.thesquare. dk • ⑧⑧⑧*

6 Hotel Fox
Check out the rooms in this cool, quirky hotel. Each has been decorated by one of 21 international artists to reflect a different mood, rather like sleeping in a modern art gallery. It caters to a young clientele, and there is a sushi and cocktail bar. ⑨ *Map G4 • Jarmers Plads 3 • 33 13 30 00 • www. hotelfox.dk • ⑧⑧⑧*

7 Axel Hotel Guldsmeden
Part of the Guldsmeden group, this boutique hotel is a surprising find in this area close to the main train station. Relax in the saunas and steam baths of the hotel spa and enjoy organic breakfasts in the heated courtyard. ⑨ *Map G6 • Helgolands-gade 11 • 33 31 32 66 • www.hotelguldsmeden. dk • ⑧⑧⑧*

8 First Hotel Kong Frederik
There have been inns and hotels on this site since the 14th century, but this hotel dates back to 1868. Extensively renovated in 2010, this classic, English-style 4-star hotel also offers a secluded courtyard lounge around the back. ⑨ *Map H4 • Vester Voldgade 25 • 33 12 59 02 • www.firsthotels.com • ⑧⑧⑧*

9 Radisson Blu Scandinavia
With 542 rooms and suites, this is Denmark's biggest hotel, offering great views of Christianshavn and the city. Its world-class facilities include Copenhagen's only casino and four restaurants – check out the 25th floor Dining Room, with panoramic views across the Øresund. ⑨ *Map J6 • Amager Boulevard 70 • 33 96 50 00 • www. radissonblu.com • ⑧⑧⑧*

10 Radisson Blu Falconer
Smaller than the other two Radisson hotels in the city, this bright and airy hotel offers a wide range of services and conveniences. It is primarily aimed at business travellers and even has a conference centre next door. ⑨ *Map B4 • Falkoner Allé 9 • 38 15 80 01 • www.radissonblu. com • ⑧⑧⑧*

Recommend your favourite hotel on traveldk.com

Left **Hotel Danmark** Right **Avenue Hotel**

TOP 10 Mid-Range Hotels

1 Carlton Hotel Guldsmeden

This hotel is about halfway down Vesterbrogade. Sophisticated yet relaxed, it has an ethnic decor with dark-wood furniture, white-washed walls and Egyptian cotton sheets. It offers delicious organic breakfasts. The hotel is a short distance from the main station. ✆ Map C5 • Vesterbrogade 66 • 33 22 15 00 • www. hotelguldsmeden.dk • ⑥⑥

2 Clarion Collection Hotel Mayfair

Close to the city's main attractions, this comfortable hotel is furnished mainly in an English style with a hint of the oriental. ✆ Map G6 • Helgolandsgade 3 • 70 12 17 00 • www.choicehotels. dk • ⑥⑥⑥

3 Hotel Danmark

This contemporary 3-star hotel is set inside an 18th-century building. It offers baby-sitting services and free Internet access in all rooms. Look out for good web weekend deals. ✆ Map H5 • Vester Voldgade 89 • 33 11 48 06 • www.hotel-danmark.dk • ⑥⑥⑥

4 Hotel Centrum

This 3-star hotel is part of the DGI-Byen group. One of the perks of staying at this hotel is that guests are allowed free entry to the DGI-Byen swimming centre and spa, which is located only a short walk away from the hotel (see p45). ✆ Map G6 • Helgolandsgade 14 • 33 31 31 11 • www.dgi-byen. dk/hotel_centrum • ⑥⑥

5 Ibsens Hotel

All rooms are non-smoking and individually decorated in this friendly hotel. It has a beautiful courtyard and offers good facilities. ✆ Map G3 • Vendersgade 23 • 33 13 19 13 • www.ibsenshotel. dk • ⑥⑥⑥

6 Comfort Hotel Esplanaden

In a peaceful location close to the green area of Kastellet (see p78) and not far from the Little Mermaid (see p9) and Amalienborg (see pp20–21), this hotel is housed inside a 19th-century building. Services include free organic coffee and a 24-hour snack bar. ✆ Map L2 • Bredgade 78 • 33 48 10 00 • www.choicehotels. dk • ⑥⑥⑥

7 Christian IV

Ideally located away from the busy city centre, this 3-star hotel is a stone's throw away from Kongens Have and Rosenborg Slot (see pp20–21). There are a range of great free services on offer, including coffee or tea and snacks served through the day and entry to the gym on Adelsgade. Check for the best prices. ✆ Map K3 • Dronningens Tværgade 45 • 33 32 10 44 • www. hotelchristianiv.dk • ⑥⑥

8 Avenue Hotel

This independent boutique hotel is located on the edge of Frederiksberg, close to both the Lakes (see p44) and the lively Nørrebro district. A hotel since 1939, it has since been renovated and offers child-friendly, spacious family rooms. There is even a sandpit on the terrace, where breakfasts can also be enjoyed. ✆ Map C4 • Åboulevard 29 • 35 37 31 11 • www.avenuehotel.dk • ⑥⑥⑥

9 First Hotel Vesterbro

This fabulous 4-star hotel has a good location on Vesterbrogade. It has large, attractive rooms with minimalist decor. There is a wonderful atrium where you can catch a bite to eat. Interestingly, in the seedier days of Vesterbro, it was the local porn cinema. ✆ Map C5 • Vesterbrogade 23–29 • 33 78 80 00 • www.firsthotels. dk/vesterbro • ⑥⑥⑥

10 Tivoli Hotel

This high-rise hotel opened in 2010. There are indoor and outdoor activities for kids, as well as a swimming pool and fitness centre. Part of the Tivoli Congress Center, it also caters for business guests. A free shuttle bus operates between the hotel and Tivoli. ✆ Map D6 • Kalvebod Brygge • www. tivolihotel.com • ⑥⑥⑥

Price Categories

For a standard,
double room per
night (with breakfast
if included), taxes
and extra charges.

⑧	up to Dkr750
⑧⑧	750–1,000
⑧⑧⑧	1,000–1,300
⑧⑧⑧⑧	1,300–1,800
⑧⑧⑧⑧⑧	over Dkr1,800

Hotel Copenhagen

TOP 10 Budget Hotels

1 Comfort Hotel Østerport

This modern hotel is a short walk away from Kastellet (see p78) and the Little Mermaid (see p9). It offers 24-hour reception, Wi-Fi and organic breakfasts (for a little extra on the room charge). ⑧ Map K1 • Oslo Plads 5 • 70 12 46 46 • www.choicehotels. dk • ⑧⑧

2 Norlandia Star Hotel

Owned by the Norlandia group, this is another centrally located hotel. It is a reasonably-priced option for the traveller on a budget. ⑧ Map G6 • Colbjørnsensgade 13 • 33 22 11 00 • www.star/ norlandiahotels.dk • ⑧

3 WakeUp Copenhagen

Designed by Kim Utzon, this ultra budget, two-star budget hotel is located along the waterfront, close to Fisketorvet shopping centre. Its 510 rooms are spread over 12 floors, with prices rising per floor. ⑧ Map D6 • Carsten Niebuhrs Gade 11 • 44 80 00 10 • www. wakeupcopenhagen.dk • ⑧

4 Hotel Sct. Thomas

A family-run hotel, Sct. Thomas is located in a quiet residential area, yet close to Vesterbro and Værnedamsvej (see p86). The cosy rooms come with shared or private bathrooms and breakfast is included.

⑧ Map C5 • Frederiksberg Allé 7 • 33 21 64 64 • www. hotelsctthomas.dk • ⑧

5 Absalon Annex

A 1-star annex of Hotel Absalon, this hotel offers clean rooms with TVs, sinks and shared bathrooms down the hallways. Free Internet access and a buffet breakfast is included. ⑧ Map G6 • Helgolandsgade 15 • 33 24 22 11 • www.absalon-hotel.dk • ⑧

6 Cab Inn City

Based on the idea of a ship's cabin, the rooms at Cab Inn City are small but perfectly designed, with all the modern conveniences tucked into a clever storage design. You can pick from bunk beds in twin rooms, double rooms and family rooms. The hotel has a pleasant ambience and offers good buffet breakfasts. ⑧ Map H6 • City Mitchellsgade 14 • 33 46 16 16 • Dis access • www. cabinn.com • ⑧

7 Cab Inn Copenhagen Express

This 3-star hotel in the popular chain is just a 12-minute walk from Rådhuspladsen, situated on the other side of the reservoirs. If you walk down the road and look across the water, you will be able to see the Tycho Brahe Planetarium (see p84). ⑧ Map C4 • Danasvej 32, Frederiksberg • 33 21 04 00 • www.cabinn.com • ⑧

8 Cab Inn Scandinavia

This Cab Inn hotel is located just a block away from the Cab Inn Copenhagen Express and a road before the Peblinge Lake. It is equipped with all the modern conveniences found at the other three Cab Inns in the city. ⑧ Map C4 • Vodroffsvej 55, Frederiksberg • 35 36 11 11 • www.cabinn.com • ⑧

9 Cab Inn Metro

The Cab Inn Metro is the fourth hotel in the city's budget Cab Inn concept, and is Denmark's largest hotel. It is located close to the airport and Fields shopping centre. All 709 rooms are modern and clean with en-suite facilities. Free wireless Internet access is included in the price. ⑧ Arne Jakobsens Allé 2 • 32 46 57 00 • www. cabinn.com • ⑧

10 Hotel Copenhagen

Just minutes away from the city centre by Metro, this hotel offers rooms sleeping up to four with shared bathrooms. There are also some rooms with en-suite facilities. Free Internet is available in the reception and breakfast can be ordered when you book for a small additional charge. ⑧ Map E6 • Egilsgade 33, Islands Brygge • 32 96 27 27 • www.hotelcopenhagen. dk • ⑧

Left **Dansk Bed and Breakfast** Right **Adina Apartment Hotel**

Other Accommodation

1 Danhostel Copenhagen Amager

Four kilometres from the city centre (20 mins by bus), this hostel offers rooms with 2–5 beds, a kitchen, laundry services, Internet access, a TV room, lockers and a children's playground. It is very close to Fields shopping centre. A YHA membership card is required. Ⓝ *Vejlands Allé 200, Sundbyvester • 32 52 29 08 • Open 2 Jan–15 Dec; Check-in: 1–5pm • Dis access • www.copenhagen youthhostel.dk • Ⓚ*

2 Danhostel Copenhagen Downtown

Located right in the heart of the city, this hostel promises a vibrant and artistic international atmosphere. It has a café, lounge and restaurant. In addition to the dorm and four-bedded rooms, there are rooms for two to three people with en-suite facilities. A YHA membership card is required, which can be bought when checking in. Ⓝ *Map J5 • Vandkunsten 5 • 70 23 21 10 • www. copenhagendowntown.com • Ⓚ*

3 Sleep In Green

Located in trendy Nørrebro, with good public transport links, this hostel has an eco-friendly outlook (hence "In Green"). It uses only organic and recyclable materials and is also into electricity and water conservation. A good place to meet other travellers. Ⓝ *Map D3 • Ravnsborggade 18, Nørrebro • 35 37 77 77 • Open end May–end Oct; Reception: 4pm–noon • Ⓚ*

4 YMCA Interpoint

Open only for a short time in the summer, this small hostel (36 beds) is very popular. It is set inside an old house and has a large living room with a piano. The rooms, though small, offer a good garden view and free Internet access. Ⓝ *Map C5 • Valdemarsgade 15, Vesterbro • 33 31 15 74 • Open Jul–mid-Aug • www. ymca-interpoint.dk • Ⓚ*

5 City Camp

Centrally located and close to the harbour, this is a good option if you want to park your camper van or caravan while in the city. To make reservations via e-mail *(see below)*, provide them your license plate number and your arrival and departure dates. Ⓝ *Fisketorvet / Vasbygade, Vesterbro • 21 42 53 84 • Open 1 Jun–1 Sep • Reservations@citycamp.dk • www.citycamp.dk • Ⓚ*

6 Bellahøj Camping

If you wish to pitch a tent, this is the nearest campsite to town. It is in a residential area, 4.5 km (2.5 miles) from the city centre on the 2A bus or a short bike ride. It provides all the basic amenities that are required while camping. Ⓝ *Hvidkildevej 66 • 38 10 11 50 • Open 1 Jun–31 Aug • www.bellahoj-camping. dk • Ⓚ*

7 Adina Apartment Hotel

Slightly away from the city centre, this apartment hotel offers great facilities, including a gym, baby-sitting services, an indoor heated pool, flat screen TVs and CD players. Ⓝ *Amerika Plads 7 • 39 69 10 00 • www.adina. eu.com • ⓀⓀⓀ*

8 Citilet

These smart, tastefully-decorated hotel suites and serviced apartments are located in the city centre. A maid service is available. Minimum stay is one month. Ⓝ *Map J4 • Brolægger-stræde 3 • 70 22 21 29 • www.citilet.dk • ⓀⓀⓀ*

9 Dansk Bed & Breakfast

This B&B agency offers good quality private accommodation in central locations. Ⓝ *Map G4 • Sankt Peders Stræde 41 • 39 61 04 05 • www.bbdk. dk • Ⓚ*

10 The Hospitality Club

Stay for free and meet a global network of hosts, travellers and locals who aim to increase intercultural understanding. Ⓝ *www. hospitalityclub.org*

Price Categories

For a standard, double room per night (with breakfast if included), taxes and extra charges.

Ⓢ	up to Dkr750
ⓈⓈ	750–1,000
ⓈⓈⓈ	1,000–1,300
ⓈⓈⓈⓈ	1,300–1,800
ⓈⓈⓈⓈⓈ	over Dkr1,800

eft **Admiral** Centre **Scandic Copenhagen**

⑩ Rooms With A View

① Radisson Blu Royal Hotel

This famous Radisson Hotel, designed by Arne Jacobsen in the 1950s, is packed with 5-star comforts. The rooms afford great views over the city. On the 20th floor, the well-known Alberto K restaurant serves a fusion of Nordic and Italian cuisine *(see p83)*. Ⓢ Map G5 • ⓈⓈⓈⓈ

② Copenhagen Island

This state-of-the-art hotel is on an island in the middle of Copenhagen harbour. Architect Kim Utzon's extraordinary building places a great emphasis on the play of glass and light. The rooms offer scenic views of the Sound. It also has its own fitness centre. Ⓢ Map J6 • Kalvebod Brygge 53 • 33 38 96 00 • www.copen hagenisland.com • ⓈⓈⓈ

③ Copenhagen Strand

This 3-star hotel is housed in a 1869 harbour-front warehouse, tucked away on a pretty, quiet street opposite the Christianshavn canal. The decor is rustic and the view is wonderful. Ⓢ Map L4 • Havnegade 37 • 33 48 99 00 • www.copenhagen strand.com • ⓈⓈⓈ

④ Admiral

Originally an 18th-century granary, the rooms in this splendid 4-star hotel overlook the Sound and offer a stunning view of the Opera House *(see p8)*. Two cannons guard the entrance and the foyer displays some beautiful models of ships. The rooms are very comfortable and the restaurant, Salt, is excellent. Ⓢ Map L3 • Toldbodgade 24–28 • 33 74 14 14 • www. admiralhotel.dk • ⓈⓈⓈⓈ

⑤ Hotel CPHLIVING

The world's first floating hotel is located in a boat on the harbour. There are just 12 rooms, all with small balconies and wireless Internet. A sun deck with deck chairs is available for guests. This is a non-smoking hotel. Ⓢ Map J6 • Langebrogade 1C • 61 60 85 46 • www. cphliving.com • ⓈⓈ

⑥ Scandic Copenhagen

Standing tall near the Tycho Brahe Planetarium *(see p84)*, it offers magnificent panoramic views over Copenhagen's rooftops. Try out their fabulous breakfasts. For the best rates, check the "Early" and "Flex" deals. Ⓢ Map C5 • Vester Søgade 6 • 33 14 35 35 • www. scandic-hotels.com/ copenhagen • ⓈⓈⓈⓈ

⑦ Danhostel Copenhagen City

This modern 5-star Danhostel is one of the biggest in the city. It is located close to Tivoli and Rådhuspladsen and offers great views over the city's attractions. Ⓢ Map C5 • HC Andersen Blvd 50 • 33 11 85 85 • Dis access • www.danhostel. dk/copenhagencity • Ⓢ

⑧ Skovshoved Hotel

Away from the bustle of central Copenhagen, this elegant seaside hotel is over 350 years old. Tastefully decorated in a Scandinavian style, it is surrounded by fishermen's houses and offers beautiful views. The restaurant is mentioned in the Michelin Guide. Ⓢ Strandvejen 267, Charlottenlund • 39 64 00 28 • www.skovshovedhotel.dk • ⓈⓈⓈ

⑨ Skodsborg Kurhotel and Spa

Formerly a summer palace, this century-old health resort is a beautiful place to stay. Overlooking the sea, it is the perfect destination for health and fitness fanatics, offering a range of therapies and fitness programmes. Ⓢ Skodsborg Strandvej 139, Skodsborg • 45 58 58 00 • www. skodsborg.dk/uk • ⓈⓈⓈⓈ

⑩ Dragør Badehotel

This 3-star harbour hotel in the fishing village of Dragør is a popular destination with tourists and boasts rooms with gorgeous views of the sea and the countryside. Ⓢ Drogdensvej 43, Dragør • 32 53 05 00 • www. badehotellet.dk • Ⓢ

General Index

Index

Acknowledgments

The Author

Antonia Cunningham would like to thank the following for their help and support while researching and writing this book:
Henrik Thierlein at Wonderful Copenhagen, Annette Wæber of Meet the Danes and Bodil and Troels Joergensen and their family for their kind hospitality; Hotel Square, No 71, Admiral Hotel, Bertrams Hotel Guldmedsen; Annette Larsen, Caroline Disum and Louise Albeck at Café Rabes Have; Mads Grimstad and Nina Wengel at the Opera House and Brian at Barcelona for their helpful advice; Nicolaj Steen Møller for his comments and advice; and all the staff who kindly showed me around hotels and restaurants and provided information. I would also especially like to thank Nick Simpson, Susan Hazledine, my sister Francesca Mitchell and my editor Fay Franklin, who was very understanding of my pregnant state and the odd delay that went with it.

Photographer Jon Spaull

Fact checking and additional text Jane Graham, Nikolaj Steen Møller, Laura Pilgaard Rasmussen

AT DORLING KINDERSLEY

Publisher Douglas Amrine

Publishing Manager Scarlett O'Hara

Design Manager Karen Constanti

Senior Cartographic Designer Casper Morris

Senior Editor Fay Franklin

Project Editor Alastair Laing

DTP Designer Natasha Lu

DK Picture Library Romaine Werblow, Rose Horridge

Senior Picture Researchers Taiyaba Khatoon, Ellen Root

Picture Researchers Marta Bescos, Sumita Khatwan, Rhiannon Furbear

Production Linda Dare

AT CREATIVE QUOTIENT
(A Repro Enterprise)

Art Director Asha Madhavan

Editors Shantala Bellare, Gauri Kelkar

Designer Dinesh Kashyap, Conrad Van Dyk

Project Managers Deepali Salvi, Jatin Mehta

Additional Editorial and Design Emma Anacootee, Simon Davis, Lydia Halliday, Integrated Publishing Solutions, Priya Kukadia, Alison McGill, Helen Peters, Sylvia Tombesi-Walton

Additional Photography Dorota and Mariusz Jarymowiczowie, Demetrio Carrasco

Picture Credits

t=top; tc=top centre; tr=top right; cla=centre left above; ca=centre above; cra=centre right above; cl=centre left; c=centre; cr=centre right; clb=centre left below; cb=centre below; crb=centre right below; bl=bottom left; bc=bottom centre; br=bottom right.

Every effort has been made to trace the copyright holders, and we apologise in advance for any unintentional omissions. We would be pleased to insert the appropriate acknowledgments in any subsequent edition of this publication.

The Publisher would like to thank the following for their kind assistance and permission to photograph their establishments: 2nd Birkegade, Amalienborg Slot, Birger Christensen, Café Ketchup, Café Ultimo, Centralhjørnet, Christiansborg Slot, Christians Kirke, Club Mambo, Copenhagen Admiral Hotel, Copenhagen Jazz House, Copenhagen Zoo, Culture Box, Danmarks Akvarium, Dansk Jødisk Museum, Designer Zoo, Det Nationalhistoriske Museum på Frederiksborg Slot, Hillerød, Emmerys, Experimentarium, Forme B, Frederiks Kirke (Marmorkirken), Gefährlich, Guinness World Records Museum, Hotel Fox, Illums Bolighus, Jailhouse Event Bar/

Restaurant, Kunstindustrimuseet, La Glace, Louisiana Museum, Magasin du Nord, Masken Bar & Café, Mojo Blues Bar, Museum Erotica, Nationalmuseet, Ny Carlsberg Glyptotek, Opera House, Orlogsmuseet, Pussy Galore's Flying Circus, Rosenborg Slot, Roskilde Museum, Rundetårn, Sneaky Fox, Søpavillonen, Sofiekælderen, Søstrene Olsen, Tage Anderson, Teatermuseet i Hofteatret, Thé à la Menthe, The Laundromat Café, The Paul, The Square Copenhagen, Tivoli, Vikingeskibsmuseet, Vor Frue Kirke, Zoo Bar.

Works of art have been reproduced with the kind permission of the following copyright holders:
Louise Bourgeois, *Eyes* (1997) © DACS, London/VAGA, New York 101tl; Henry Moore, *Two Piece Reclining Figure No. 5, 1963-64* (LH 517) © The Henry Moore Foundation 101tr.

The publisher would like to thank the following individuals, companies and picture libraries for their kind permissions to reproduce their photographs:

4CORNERS IMAGES:
SIME / Mezzanotte Susy 94–5.

ALAMY: Meritzo 109tl; nagelestock. com 72–3; AVENUE HOTEL: 114tr.

COPENHAGEN JAZZ HOUSE: 70tl; CORBIS: Archivo Iconografico, S.A. 33tl, 33tr.

DANSK DESIGN CENTER: 62cra; DK IMAGES: David Borland 96tr; Rough

Guides/Helena Smith 66tl.

ECO EGO: 80tl.

FREDERIKSBORG SLOT: Larsen Lennart 32t; Hans Petersen 32br.

HOTEL COPENHAGEN: 115tl.

INTOXICA BAR -TIKI BAR & KITCHEN: 70tr

OLDŘICH KARASEK: 20–21c.

LONELY PLANET IMAGES:
Anders Blomqvist 60–61.

MO CHRISTIANSHAVN: 92tl.

NATIONALMUSEET: 7clb, 26cr, 26br, 27tl, 27bl, 27cra; NIKOLAJ STEEN MØLLER: 71tl; NY CARLSBERG GLYPTOTEK: 24cb, 25clb.

ORDRUPGAARD: 96tl.

ROSENBORG SLOT: 15ca, 74tl; RUST: 51br, 81tl.

STATENS MUSEUM FOR KUNST: 22c, 22bc, 23tr, 23c.

SUPERSTOCK:
Brian Lawrence 4–5.

TIVOLI: 10–11c, 43tl.

VISIT DENMARK: 3bl, 38tc, 10cla; Ireneusz Cyranek 34tr; Danmarks Turistrad 102tl; Bob Krist 34bl; Nicolai Perjesi 34tc; Ukendt 6ca.

WONDERFUL COPENHAGEN: 70tr, 107tr, 116tr, 117c.

All other images © Dorling Kindersley.

For further information see:
www.dkimages.com.

Acknowledgments

Special Editions of DK Travel Guides

DK Travel Guides can be purchased in bulk quantities at discounted prices for use in promotions or as premiums. We are also able to offer special editions and personalized jackets, corporate imprints, and excerpts from all of our books, tailored specifically to meet your own needs.

To find out more, please contact:

(in the US) **SpecialSales@dk.com**

(in the UK) **travelspecialsales@uk. dk.com**

(in Canada) DK Special Sales at **general@tourmaline.ca**

(in Australia) **business.development@ pearson.com.au**

Phrase Book

In an Emergency

Help!	**Hjælp!**	yellb!
Stop!	**Stands!**	stanns!
Can you call a doctor?	**Kan du ringe til en læge?**	kann do ringe-til ehn laiyeh?
Can you call an ambulance?	**Kan du ringe til en ambulance?**	kann do ringe-til ehn ahm-boo-lang-seh?
Can you call the police?	**Kan du ringe til politiet?**	kann do ringe-til po-ly-tee'd?
Can you call the fire brigade?	**Kan du ringe til brandvæsenet?**	kann do ringe-til brahn-vaiys-ned?
Is there a telephone here?	**Er der en telefon i nærheden?**	e-ah dah ehn tele-fohn ee neya-hethen?
Where is the nearest hospital?	**Hvor er det nærmeste hospital?**	voa e-ah deh neh-meste hoh-spee-tahl

Useful Phrases

Sorry	**Undskyld**	ons-gull
Goodnight	**Godnat**	goh-nad
Goodbye	**Farvel**	fah-vell
Good evening	**Godaften**	goh-ahf-tehn
Good morning	**Godmorgen**	goh-moh'n
Good morning (after about 9am)	**Goddag**	goh-dah
Yes	**Ja**	yah
No	**Nej**	nye
Please	**Værsgo/ Velbekomme**	vehs-goh/ vell-beh-commeh
Thank you	**Tak**	tahgg
How are you?	**Hvordan har du det?/ Hvordan går det?**	voh-dann hah do deh?/ voh-dan go deh?
Well, thank you	**Godt, tak**	gohd, tahgg
Pleased to have met you	**Det var rart at møde dig**	deh vah rahd add meuthen die
See you!	**Vi ses!**	vee sehs!
I understand	**Jeg forstår**	yay fuh-stoah
I don't understand	**Jeg forstår ikke**	yay fuh-stoah egge
Does anyone speak English?	**Er der nogen, der kan tale engelsk?**	e-ah dah noh-enn dah kann tah-leh eng-ellsgg?
good	**god**	guth
bad	**dårlig**	doh-lee
up	**op**	ohb
down	**ned**	neth
near	**tæt på**	taid poh
far	**langt fra**	lahngd fra
on the left	**til venstre**	till vehn-streh
on the right	**til højre**	till hoy-reh
open	**åben**	oh-ben
closed	**lukket**	luh-geth
warm	**varm**	vahm
cold	**kold**	koll
big	**stor**	stoah
little	**lille**	lee-leh

Making a Telephone Call

Whom am I speaking to?	**Hvem taler jeg med?**	vemm talah yay meth?
I would like to call...	**Jeg vil gerne ringe til...**	yay vill geh-neh ring-eh till...
I will telephone again	**Jeg ringer en gang til**	yay ring-ah ehn gahng till

In a Hotel

Do you have double rooms?	**Findes her dobbelt-værelser?**	feh-ness he-ah dob-belld vah-hel-sah?
With bathroom	**Med bade-værelse**	meth bah-the-vah-hel-sah
With washbasin	**Med hånd-vask**	meth hohn-vasgg
key	**nøgle**	noy-leh
I have a reservation	**Jeg har en reservation**	yay hah ehn res-sah-vah-shohn

Sightseeing

entrance	**indgang**	ehn-gahng
exit	**udgang**	ooth-gahng
exhibition	**udstilling**	ooth-stelling
tourist information	**turisto-plysning**	tooh-reesd-ohb-lehs-ning
town/city hall	**rådhus**	rahd-hus
post office	**posthus**	posd-hus
cathedral	**domkirke**	dom-kia-keh
church	**kirke**	kia-keh
museum	**museum**	muh-seh-uhm
town bus	**bybus**	bih-boos
long-distance bus	**rutebil**	roo-teh-beel
railway station	**banegård**	bah-neh-goh
airport	**lufthavn**	luhft-havn
train	**tog**	toh
ferry terminal	**færgehavn**	fah-veh-havn
bus stop	**busstoppested**	buhs-sdob-beh-steth
long-distance bus station	**rutebilstation**	roo-teh-beel-sta-shion
a public toilet	**et offentligt toilet**	ehd off-end-ligd toa-led

Shopping

I wish to buy...	**Jeg vil gerne købe...**	yay vill geh-neh kyh-beh...
Do you have...?	**Findes der...?**	feh-ness de-ah...?
How much does it cost?	**Hvad koster det?**	vath koh-stah deh
expensive	**dyr**	dyh-ah
cheap	**billig**	billy
size	**størrelse**	stoh-ell-seh
general store	**købmand**	keuhb-mann
greengrocer	**grønthandler**	grund-handla
supermarket	**supermarked**	suh-pah-mah-keth
market	**marked**	mah-keth

Eating Out

Do you have a table for... people?	**Har I et bord til... personer?**	hah ee ed boah til... peh-soh-nah
I would like to	**Jeg vil gerne**	yay vill geh-neh

at by the window	sidde ved vinduet	saithe veth veen-do-ed
wish to order...	Jeg vil gerne bestille...	yay vill geh-neh beh-stilleh...
n a vegetarian	Jeg er vegetar	yay eh-ah veh-gehta
...ildren's menu	børnemenu	byeh-neh-meh-nye
...ily special	dagens ret	dayens rad
...arter	forret	foh-red
...ain course	hovedret	hoh-veth-red
...essert	dessert	deh-seh'd
...ine list	vinkort	veen-cod
...weet	sødt	sodt
...ur	surt	suad
...icy	stærkt	stehgd
...ay I have / ...he bill?	Må jeg bede om regningen?	moh yay beh-theh uhm rahy-ning-ehn

Menu Decoder

...gurk	cucumber	a-guag
...nanas	pineapple	a-nah-nas
...ppelsin	orange	abbel-seen
...lomme	plum	blum-ma
...rød	bread	bruth
...hampignon	mushroom	sham-pee-ong
...anskvand	mineral water	dansg vann
...ersken	peach	fes-gehn
...sk	fish	fesgg
...ade	cream	flu-theh
...ulerod	carrot	gooleh-roth
...rontsager	vegetables	grunn-saha
...ummer	lobster	humma
	ice cream	ees
...affe	coffee	kah-feh
...artofler	potatoes	kah-toff-lah
...ød	meat	kuth
...ylling	chicken	killing
...ål	cabbage	kohl
...aks	salmon	lahggs
...m	lamb	lahm
...everpostej	liver paté	leh-vah-poh-stie
...øg	onion	loy
...ælk	milk	mailgg
...ksekød	beef	ogg-seh-kuth
...st	cheese	ossd
...eber	pepper	peh-ba
...ore	leek	po-a
...urløj	chives	poo-a-loy
...ølse	sausage	pill-seh
...ejer	shrimps	rah-yah
...s	rice	rees
...adspætte	plaice	roth-speh-da
...øget fisk	smoked fish	roy-heth fesgg
...aftevand	squash	sah-fteh-vann
...alat	salad	sah-lad
...alt	salt	sald
...ild	herring	sil
...kaldyr	shellfish	sgall-dya
...kinke	ham	sgeng-geh
...mør	butter	smuah
...odavand	fizzy drink	sodah-vann
...teg	steak	stie
...vinekød	pork	svee-neh-kuth
...yltetøj	jam	sill-teh-toi
...e	tea	teh
...ærte	quiche/pie	te-ah-teh

torsk	cod	tohsgg
vand	water	vann
wienerbrød	Danish pastry	vee-nah-bryd
æble	apple	eh-bleh
æg	egg	egg
øl	beer	uhl

Time

today	i dag	ee-day
tomorrow	i morgen	ee-mohn
yesterday	i går	ee-goh
before noon	formiddag	foh-medday
afternoon	eftermiddag	ehftah-medday
evening	aften	ahftehn
night	nat	nadd
minute	minut	meh-nude
hour	time	tee-meh
week	uge	oo-eh
month	måned	moe-neth
year	år	oah

Days of the Week

Monday	mandag	mann-day
Tuesday	tirsdag	teahs-day
Wednesday	onsdag	uns-day
Thursday	torsdag	toahs-day
Friday	fredag	frey-day
Saturday	lørdag	lur-day
Sunday	søndag	son-day

Months

January	januar	ya-nuah
February	februar	fib-buah
March	marts	mahds
April	april	apreal
May	maj	mai
June	juni	yoo-nee
July	juli	yoo-lee
August	august	auw-guhsd
September	september	sehb-tern-bah
October	oktober	ogg-toh-bah
November	november	noh-vem-bah
December	december	deh-sem-bah

Numbers

0	nul	noll
1	en	ehn
2	to	toh
3	tre	tray
4	fire	fee-ah
5	fem	femm
6	seks	seggs
7	syv	siu
8	otte	oh-deh
9	ni	nee
10	ti	tee
20	tyve	tyh-veh
30	tredive	traith-veh
40	fyrre	fyr-reh
50	halvtreds	hahl-traiths
60	tres	traiths
70	halvfjerds	hahl-fyads
80	firs	fee-ahs
90	halvfems	hahl-femms
100	hundrede	hoon-dreh-the
200	tohundrede	toh-hoon-dreh-the
1,000	tusind	tooh-sin-deh
2,000	totusinde	toh-tooh-sin-deh

Selected Street Index